TRADITIONAL
MOROCCAN
COOKING

Madame Guinaudeau,
a Frenchwoman
married to a doctor
practicing in Fez,
lived for more than
three decades in
the city where she
researched
and wrote this book.

6-12 (18)   8,715
(21)

3-

D1456829

TRADITIONAL MOROCCAN COOKING

Recipes from Fez

Z. Guinaudeau

Translated from the French by
J. E. Harris

Decorations by J. E. Laurent

Serif

London

This edition first published 2003 by
Serif
47 Strahan Road
London E3 5DA

Originally published in 1994.
First published in Rabat by J. E. Laurent as *Fès vu par sa cuisine* in 1958 and as
Fez: Traditional Moroccan Cooking Book, translated by J. E. Harris, in 1964

British Library Cataloging in Publication Data.
A catalogue record for this book
is available from the British Library

Library of Congress Cataloging-in-Publication Data.
A catalog record for this book
is available from the Library of Congress

ISBN 1 897959 43 5

Designed by Ralph Barnby
Typeset in Liverpool by Derek Doyle & Associates
Printed and bound in Malta by Gutenburg Press Ltd.

To my Fassi friends who taught me to understand and love their scented and colourful cuisine.

To those whose inspiration created these refined and striking dishes.

CONTENTS

CONTENTS

CONTENTS

CONTENTS

CONTENTS

FOREWORD

When years ago I travelled to research Morocco's cooking, Madame Guinaudeau was mentioned to me by everybody I met and I talked to several people who boasted that they had given her recipes. They all spoke of her with affection and respect. Today, although a number of books have appeared on the subject of their country's cuisine, a younger generation of Moroccans has the greatest respect for Madame Guinaudeau's *Fès Vu par sa Cuisine*, first published in 1958 and translated here as *Traditional Moroccan Cooking: Recipes from Fez*. That the most exclusive restaurant in Fez has been called Fès Vu par sa Cuisine is an indication of the high regard in which the book is held. Moroccans are immensely proud of their cuisine and rightly regard it as one of the best in the world, so for a foreign author to be so highly esteemed by them is no small accolade.

By all accounts the book was the first on Moroccan cooking since an anonymous compilation of Maghrebi and Andalusian recipes appeared in Arabic in Spain in the twelfth century. (As her book went off to press Madame Guinaudeau added a note that she had thought she was the first person to write about Moroccan food, but that after writing it she heard that a work by John, 4th Marquis of Bute, entitled *Moorish Recipes* was published in Edinburgh in 1955.) That is merit in itself, but the book is also remarkable in many other ways. There is in Madame Guinaudeau's writing a truth and authenticity which is rarely found in cookery books. Every recipe, every description, every detail of people's lives which she gives is the result of her own observation, which makes her book completely original and absolutely unique; there is passion and enthusiasm which comes through in every page.

Perhaps it is because she was an outsider that she had such a fascination with and respect for her subject, and also a concern to avoid the phoney. The wife of a French doctor – a much-loved eye specialist – she moved to Fez in 1929 and lived there for more than three decades. She made it her joy to pursue recipes and culinary information in the kitchens of Fez, which became her beloved city. It was also a way of getting to know the people. She was invited to eat and to watch the cooking operations in modest and grand homes in the *casbah* and the *medina* as well as in the palaces of aristocratic families, in ethnic communities like the Jews in the *mellah* (the city's old Jewish quarter) and primitive Berber villages outside the city.

The book took her twenty years to research. Ahmed Sefrioui wrote in the preface to the first edition that it was a contribution to the history of his country, a document of great human interest. Madame Guinaudeau described the way people lived and entertained, the protocol of their banquets, the activities of the kitchen and the public bakehouse, and brought a whole mysterious world to life. She said she wanted to make the sparkle of the copper pots sing for us and to let us feel the rustic textures of the clay and the wood, and she succeeded. We can feel what it is like to sit in an indoor courtyard with turquoise and cobalt tiles and water running from a fountain, the scent of jasmine mingling with the smells of a stew simmering in the burning midday sun, and what it is like to pass a spice shop in the souk and see the seeds and pods and contorted pieces of bark and piles of spices and rosebuds while the mingled smells hang like a thread around the warren of narrow streets.

Her second, much larger book, *Les Secrets des Cuisines en Terre Marocaine* on the regional cooking of Morocco, published in France in 1981 under her full name Zette Guinaudeau-Franc, incorporates the entire first book. She explains that the dishes of Fez have such a major place in it because they are the country's most refined. Fez is indeed famous for her cooking. It is an immensely varied and surprising cuisine which mixes ginger and hot chilli pepper with honey and sugar and marries meat with fruit. It is colourful and aromatic and makes use of a very long list of spices which are always used with a delicate hand. The Arab cooking of Baghdad during the Abbassid Caliphate, Andalusian styles brought back by the returning Moors after the Catholic Reconquista of Spain, Ottoman Turkish specialities arrived through the occupation of Tetuan, ingredients from Africa and of course the old traditions of the indigenous Berbers all played their part in creating this prestigious cuisine.

Madame Guinaudeau's ambition was to fix the cooking traditions of Fez before they were transformed by contact with Europe. Now that Moroccan cuisine has become fashionable and is appreciated as one of the tastiest and most sophisticated of the Mediterranean, her work is more important than ever. Of course we do not want to spend hours in the kitchen as they did decades ago in Morocco, and we will make things easier for ourselves with pre-cooked packet *couscous* and our own short-cuts, but we need to know without simplification or embellishment how the real thing was and still is in most Moroccan homes. *Traditional Moroccan Cooking: Recipes from Fez* is a classic of lasting value which brings it all to us in a most engaging way.

Claudia Roden

PREFACE

Moroccans have the right to be proud of their cooking, for there cannot be any doubt that this art reflects the degree of a nation's civilisation. Dishes carefully and cleverly prepared, as pleasing to the eye as to the taste, contribute not only to our physical well-being but often have a most happy effect on our temper. The deepest depression vanishes at the sight of a really good meal.

Moroccan cuisine takes its place among the world's most savoury and refined. In Moroccan cooking, as with other cuisines, one must distinguish between two sorts of dishes, those which are intended for important banquets, and are the work of professional chefs, and more modest ones which are cooked with loving care by the lady of the house.

Madame Guinaudeau has had the merit of arranging a most accurate list of recipes in use in Fez. She has tried out these recipes herself and made the most meticulous notes about both the preparation and the ingredients. Her book is not only compiled for the good housewife, it is a contribution to the history of this country and a document of great human interest. We know that such a work requires much patient research and the gift of sympathy and enthusiasm. Madame Guinaudeau has successfully accomplished a difficult task. We owe her our warmest thanks.

Ahmed Sefrioui

AUTHOR'S FOREWORD

The time has come to fix the tradition of cooking in Fez before it becomes too Europeanised. Fassi cuisine is composed chiefly of well-cooked meat simmering in spiced sauces heavy with oil and butter, sauces in which ginger and pepper mingle with honey and sugar; the part played by fruit and vegetables is reduced to a discreet accompaniment.

This tradition, coming from the Orient with Morocco's Arabic conquerors, was impregnated, via Tetuan and Algiers, with the sweet and insipid perfume of Constantinople, passing again through Andalusia. Finally, there were added certain simple and nourishing dishes from the indigenous Berbers to produce the highly civilised cuisine to be found today among the wealthier inhabitants of Fez.

I offer this book which is the result of search and investigation, by smell, by touch and by taste, during more than twenty years among both the rich and the poor families of Fez.

The artist J.E. Laurent's witty and expressive drawings bring alive the very spirit of Fez.

In this book the weights and measures given for a British and American readership have been adapted as follows:

2 lb 4 oz = 1 kilogram
1 oz = 30 grams
2 pints = 1 litre

Table Manners
and Customs

In the street the burning June sun is at its zenith. There is constant noise and movement on all sides. Cries of '*Balek, balek*'; buying, selling, discussing; children pushing and crying; great jars of oil being carried home; donkeys stumbling along; proud, distant students passed by hurrying craftsmen; mingled smells – spices, oil, jasmine and orange blossom, remains of stale vegetables and datura. Thick dust makes a hell of the hot, crowded street.

At last the quiet passage where our host's son awaits us. The open door casts a deep, cool shadow. In one corner a mule; a few spongers up from the country chat hopefully with the door-keeper over a glass of mint tea.

A rapid walk down a narrow corridor then suddenly, after a sharp turn, the oasis, an impression of space, calm, the pure light of the great patio. Mosaics and a marble fountain, whitewashed arches, the white robes of our host. An aristocratic home where the only discreet note of colour is given by the *zellijes* or coloured tiles.

Led by the master of the house, we advance, relaxed and at ease. Impressions: glances from the

windows above, children held back in a corner by the black nurse, young women from the south, a mass of bright colours flying towards the kitchen.

The room where we are installed is long, decorated with mosaics, the ceiling coloured, the mattresses covered with brocade, the cushions embroidered in gold. On shelves facing the high door there are many clocks, all silent; chinaware; vases, Victorian or Louis Philippe, filled with paper flowers. In one corner a brass four-poster bed, throne of cushions and mattresses! In contrast to the patio, a riot of daring colours and riches. Conversation: polite formulas, health and the weather.

Before us, silently on bare feet, a ballet of young women, flowers behind their ears, skirts tucked up, hips tightly swathed in their striped cotton dresses, lays down in the patio, in front of the entrance to the dining-hall, the great dishes kept hot in their copper bowls with pointed covers.

Two servants at each angle of the painted door, caryatids beneath the raised silken curtains, wait for the master to clap his hands discreetly before beginning the ceremony of the feast.

Across the carpet the low inlaid table is wheeled towards us and we take our places on the mattresses round it after a ewer has been taken round and a trickle of perfumed water poured over three fingers of the right hand.

Seated on a cushion in the corner the master looks on. It is one of the sons of the house standing in the doorway who watches over the protocol, the changing of the dishes, water, bread. Everyone spreads a thick towel over his knees.

Yacout with arched back brings in the *bistilla*, flaky spiced pastry, frosty with sugar, shaded with cinnamon, in a huge china dish. '*Bsmillah*.' Refined and delicate, food for the gods, it is very true that the civilisation of a people can be judged by its cooking.

With thumb, forefinger and the middle finger of the right hand take a piece of stuffing or a pigeon wing from under the golden crust. Lay the clean picked bones on the table. Finally, attack the pastry which melts in the mouth with its sugar and cinnamon. Before each guest the space becomes bigger, the gesture from the dish to the lips slower, the appetite calmer, allowing for the dishes which are to follow.

A discreet snap of the fingers, in the twinkling of

an eye the *bistilla* disappears, leaving the debris of bones scattered over the table. Half a *ksra* is placed before each guest. Then Yacout brings in the *choua*, that rather insipid steamed mutton happily seasoned with cumin which rests the palate after the extraordinary spices of the previous dish. With three fingers the guest of honour searches under the shoulder blade and offers me the tenderest morsel ...

Then comes the chicken with almonds, three at least so as not to appear *mskin* or poor. Before tasting the meat, dip your bread in the terribly hot sauce which will bring a rush of blood to the head.

There follows a turkey *ma'amra*; after breaking the breast bone we enjoy the stuffing, a *qamama tagine* with a dazzling purée of onions and honey.

Finally a *couscous* to subdue our hunger. To avoid the shame of failure I shall not attempt to roll it into small pellets, the correct way to eat *couscous*. Fortunately a spoon is nearly always provided by our thoughtful hosts.

During this meal, which is typical of a simple reception, there is little conversation; that would spoil the pleasure and appreciation of each dish.

It is not seemly to offer water, which distends the stomach, but if necessary one can ask to quench one's thirst.

The meat dishes finished, the broken bones are rapidly swept away, the table cleared.

A gentle rest, then the sweet steamed semolina with a glass of cold milk, before ending with the fruits of the season.

And the ballet starts again as at the beginning of

the meal. Young women juggle away the table, then pass their hands over the carpet like a vacuum cleaner. One of them presents the silver ewer filled with warm water with which we purify our mouths, lips and hands. The cushion and the mattresses are put back in their place. Life is sweet, utterly satisfied. *Chban* or satiated, we are drunk with strong spices, heavy with sauces.

This formidable meal passes off better than one would think. In spite of the number of dishes the absence of wine allows one to digest the well-cooked meats quite easily, above all if one has the courage not to drink during the meal but to wait for the mint tea which follows.

Now the dishes, which are still far from empty, especially those served last, will be taken first to the women and children of the house, who from the first floor or across the patio behind curtains have been spying and waiting, then they will go to the kitchens, and when the porter, amidst a swarm of flies, throws the bones on the rubbish heap they are white and clean, as though they had lain in the burning desert sun.

The bourgeois families of Fez have at least thirty or forty people to feed every day. For a simple family meal only one or two *tagines* are served. An artisan is satisfied with a modest stew. Necessity renders the workman frugal: after receiving his wages he is obliged to buy himself vegetables and oil for his meal; at midday he will eat only bread and olives and his family semolina and sour milk. Never forget that the Arab working man has still the stomach of a nomad and can exist for many days on dates and dried figs, but when the occasion arises he can eat a whole sheep.

There are of course definite rules as to the succession of dishes. In giving a recipe I have generally indicated at what moment the *tagine* should be served. In the preceding pages I have given you a classical type of meal.

Remember that the *bistilla* must be served first, then the *choua*, fish, spring or summer *tagines* according to the season, *tfaia tagine*, *kefta* and *mrouzia*.

The mutton *mahammar* and *mqalli*. Chicken with lemons and olives roasted with spices. Stuffed chicken with rice, raisins and olives. *Qamama tagine* with onions and honey. Finally, a choice of the different *couscous*, rice with milk, semolina with sour milk. The *m'hanncha* or *haloua* served at marriages and circumcisions. Diversity is not lacking and, even if the basic ingredients are few, the dishes – thanks to the different spices and the imagination of the cooks – offer a variety of which the appetite never tires.

Receptions in Fez, with the courtesy of the hosts, the opulence of the surroundings, the elegance of the costumes, the Andalusian music, the dances of the *chikhat*, the conversation, and the culinary art – all combine to form the summit of a rich culture.

THE KITCHEN

On going into the kitchen of a house in Fez you are struck by the austerity of the room, far removed from the brilliant arsenal and laboratory atmosphere of the modern kitchen. In the semi-darkness, so cool in summer, so mortally damp with the rain in the winter, the cooking utensils are of glazed earthenware or copper. The *kanoun*, a movable brazier of sun-baked clay, and a few holes in a tiled kitchen stove are the only cooking apparatus. The charcoal which perfumes the brochettes and allows the sauces to simmer gently dirties and blackens the whitewashed walls and is the only form of heating.

No chairs, an old carpet folded and placed on the *zellijes* serves as a seat for the exuberant black woman, come, according to tradition since the Algerian exodus, from Tetuan, from whence emerge the most highly esteemed cooks. The young servants, babbling little parakeets, bare feet in wooden sandles, bright coloured dresses whirling around as they bustle about, ready to obey at the slightest gesture from the *dada*, queen and priestess of the kitchen. She is dressed in long multi-coloured robes tucked up in front, draped and knotted at the back, with wide sleeves held in place by a twisted silken cord; a heavy flowered bulk with a face of ebony or bronze beneath the fringed turban. Her arms and ankles are encircled by silver bracelets which tinkle at every gesture. She is complete mistress and queen in her own domain.

In the darkness of the room lit only by the red gleam of copper and charcoal, enlivened by the sound of water dripping from the fountain on to the tiles, the hammering of the pestle and mortar and the voice of the *dada* scolding the servants, one is saturated with the smell of spices, the pungency of olive oil and *smen* which rasp the throat; at the same time one is enveloped in the sweetness of sandalwood, mint and roses. In this country where time doesn't count, isn't the rusticity of the cooking apparatus the secret of these dishes so patiently prepared? Happy the town where women still have the time and taste to cook well.

In this room where empiric drugs are elaborated and *tagines* sweetened, where orange blossom is distilled and pepper ground, no gesture is ever made without first saying '*Bsmillah*' to ask for Allah's blessing.

UTENSILS FOR COOKING AND SERVING

I would like to make you see the glitter of the copper and brass pots, the colour of the baskets made from esparto grass and *doum*; praise the shape of the coarsely decorated brown and ochre pottery; have you feel the roughness of the wood, the artlessness of the earthenware, the simplicity and primitive austerity of the shapes and raw materials; and at the same time show you the rich decoration of the English and Chinese porcelain, the painted and gilded cut glass from central Europe.

Boqrej: a kettle used for boiling water for tea.

Chkoua: a goatskin bottle used for carrying water.

Chtato: a small sieve, the bottom of which is made of linen or silk spun in Fez.

Gdra: the lower part of the pot for *couscous* in which the meat and vegetables are cooked, made of earthenware or copper.

Gdra del trid: a pot with a curved bottom, and a large paunch-like opening, which, when placed on the brazier, sends the heat to the inner sides and bottom of the pot, where the sheets of dough for *trid* are cooked.

Genbura: a glazed earthenware pot, very broad relative to its height, used for keeping water.

Ghorbal: a sieve, its bottom made of perforated leather, used for gauging the semolina.

Gsaa: a large, round unglazed baked clay dish made in Fez. The *gsaa* is made of oak, olive or walnut wood in certain districts, or from palms in the oases. Used for making bread and *couscous* and kneading pastry, the *gsaa* is also employed for washing.

Ied ettas: an often charmingly shaped ewer with a long slender spout in brass or embossed silver plate, used for pouring water over the fingers before and after a meal. When not in use it is placed on a pan called a *tass*.

Kanoun: a charcoal pan made of iron or copper, but more often of sun-baked clay.

Khabia: an earthenware jar, glazed inside, high and not very wide, found in different sizes and used for preserving meat and storing dried vegetables, flour and corn.

Kskas: that part of the pot, perforated at the bottom and inserted in the *gdra*, used for cooking the *couscous* grains.

Mghorfa: a large spoon carved out of a block of wood.

Mida: in Fez they call a round dish with an odd pointed hat in which cakes are served a *mida*, a wooden tray with a high rim and a conical lid is also called a *mida*, and finally the round table on which meals are served is the *mida*.

Midouna: A flat and flexible plaited basket woven from the fibres of esparto grass or *doum*.

Mqla: flat-bottomed copper pan with a straight edge and two handles.

Nafekh: an earthenware brazier.

Qa tagine: the deep copper dish in which the *tagine slaoui* is inserted and which serves to protect the table.

Qettara: an alembic used for distilling roses and orange-blossom.

Siniya: a tray made of embossed or plain copper, brass or silver plate. Those on which the utensils for making tea are placed have legs a few inches high.

Tagine slaoui: a round dish of glazed earthenware covered with a pointed lid which fits the dish exactly and can be used for cooking, keeping the dish hot or serving the *tagine*. *Slaoui* is used as a diminutive.

Tanjir: a large cooking pot.

Taoua: a basin designed to receive dirty water. These are made of copper or embossed silver plate and covered with a slab of the same metal in the middle of which the ewer is placed. It is over this basin that hands are washed before and after meals.

Tbiqa: a stiff round basket with a pointed lid made of esparto grass or *doum* decorated with coloured leather. Manufactured in or round about Marrakesh. Bread is placed in the *tbiqa* to protect it from the dust.

Tbla or *mida*: a round cedarwood dining-table, just over a foot high; the diameter varies according to the number of guests. Those made in Fez are plain or painted; those from Mogador are of inlaid woods encrusted with mother-of-pearl and much sought after.

Tboq: a sort of *midouna* made of finer basket-work.

Tila: a sieve made of rush or wire used for separating the bran from the crushed corn.

Tobsil dettiab: a large copper-plated tray with a small straight edge, used for glazing the *bistilla*.

Tobsil dial louarqa: a tray of the same sort, but it is the outside, which is copper-plated, on which the sheets of pastry for *bistilla* are cooked.

With these utensils washing up is quickly done; the guests gone, the serving women will wash the earthenware dishes in the small pond in the middle of the patio, rubbing them with fine sand brought by some poor woman in a sack on her back from the local quarries and sold at the door for a few pence.

It is polishing them with that same sand, a lemon and a half-ripe tomato that will make the copper and brass in the kitchen glow with such power and brilliance.

POTTERY

From the hill of Dar-Mahres to the south of Fez comes the clay which makes the potters' fortune.

Near Sidi-Frej, the city's old lunatic asylum, there used to be a little place of which nothing now remains. Smelling of bitumen, it was filled with small shops, all displaying their stocks of unglazed pottery. Disdainful of the tourists' curiosity, the *mallem* or craftsman decorated the pottery with tar with the tip of his agile forefinger. For a few francs one could carry away bowls, jars, water-pots and large deep dishes. You can find these shops again today, scattered through the town. The potters are survivors of that corner of Fez which no longer exists.

Between Attarine, Fez's spice market, and the Moulay Idriss sanctuary there is an entire street, long and narrow, on each side of which the shops display Fez pottery from floor to ceiling: bowls, vases, water-pots, dishes hung on string. Facing us, deep round dishes, deep conical-shaped dishes for *couscous*, soup tureens with high lids, decorated with geometric or floral designs both naïve and skilful, plain, coloured or with polychrome designs with blue the dominating colour. That blue of Fez, sometimes a deep sea blue, sometimes shining and light, and the plain deep green of the bottles of oil: colours obtained from minerals found around Fez.

Unevenly glazed, but producing designs full of charm ... flaws you certainly find in this pottery, but sometimes too the joyous discovery of a rare piece where the spontaneity of design is allied to a fine finish.

The street is still there, the merchants sitting in their shops. One or two remain faithful to the supply of goods from the potters, the others, with an eye to the main chance, have abandoned this primitive ware for more practical European ironmongery.

* * *

Pottery from Kelaa des Sless, buttress of the Rif, is decorated with yellow ochre and brown geometric designs. Shapes of great purity. Etruscan, African or Latin American art? Material hardened and oiled so it looks like polished wood.

Water-pots, jars, pots hanging from a cord, used by the *fellah* for the melted butter which he will sell in the town. Rancid odours? Yes, but also beauty of form and material, polished, hard and shining.

SPICES

Eyes filled with the harmonious green of the Chrabline minaret, we enter the bustling atmosphere of the Attarine souk.

Berbers smelling of mutton and cloves gaze with envy at the glittering beads, the bright materials, the motley trimmings. I stop there, drunk with the scent, colour and noise, and lean against the narrow edge of a shop between a sack of scarlet pimentos and a basket of rose-buds.

It is here that I have gathered the spices that you will use in the dishes which follow. I will give you, briefly, the names in English and Arabic and what I know of the origin of each. Doubtless there are errors in this work – to give you absolutely accurate information one would have to be both a botanist and an etymologist but I am only ... a cook.

Insects, leaves, flowers, petals, seeds, roots and galls. China, India, Java, Egypt, black Africa, the gardens and valleys of Morocco, blending perfumes foreign to our European senses. Spices violent with all the wildness of the countries where they have ripened, sweet from the loving culture of the gardens where they have flowered, here is all the fascination of your

dark kitchens, the odour of your streets. Spices are the soul of Fez.

Spices and aromatic plants used in cooking which do not go to make up *ras el hanout*:

Absinthe: *chiba*, the cultivated sort can replace mint in tea.

Ambrosia: *mkhinza*.

Aniseed: *nafaa*, this can be wild or cultivated in the Tafilalet.

Basil: *hbeq zhiri*.

Caraway seed: *karoniya*, found in the region of Meknès.

Citron: *laranj*, the juice is used to acidify olives.

Cloves: *qronfel*.

Coriander: *qosbour*, both the leaves and seeds are used for seasoning.

Cumin: *kamoun*, cultivated in the region of Marrakesh.

Fennel: *bsbas*, the wild variety.

Green Spanish aniseed: *habbt hlawa*, found in the region of Meknès.

Gum mastic: *mska*.

Hemp: *kif* or hashish is used to make *majoun*.

Hot red pepper: *felfla soudania*, found in North Africa and Senegal.

Liquorice: *arqsous*, this is sucked by children and also used in cooking snails.

Mint: *nana* or *iqama*, the *mentha viridis* used in tea, the best is grown around Zerhoun, Sefrou and Meknès.

Parsley: *madnousse*.

Saffron: *zafrane*, from Sous and Spain.

Sage: *salmiya*, used as an infusion in tea.

Sesame: *jljlan*, cultivated in Chaouia.

Sharp hot red pepper: *felfla harra*, from the region of Marrakesh.

Sweet marjoram: *mrdeddouch*, perfumes the water in which snails are cooked.

Sweet red pepper, pimento or paprika: *felfla hlouwa*.

Thyme: *zatr*, abundant and scented in the mountains.

Verbena: *louiza*, an infusion.

Wild mint: *fliou*, peppermint.

RAS EL HANOUT

'The head' or 'the top' of the shop is the name given to a synthesis of spices, rose-buds and cinnamon together with pimento and black pepper. The metallic glint of the cantharide is mingled with the grey stalks of ginger and more than two dozen spices are needed to complete the intoxicating aroma in which the nomad warrior has combined all the scents of the countries he has passed through.

Ras el hanout is the spice used at Eid el Kebir, for *mrouzia*, for certain winter dishes which heat the blood and always in the cooking of game. And if it is used rather less nowadays, old men when feeling chilly in the winter still put it into *majoun*, a preparation which is supposed to warm them and restore virility.

SPICES IN RAS EL HANOUT

Cardamom: *qaqulla*, seeds from the ginger tree; from Malabar and Ceylon.

Mace: *bsiba*, the outer layer of nutmeg; from Java and Sumatra.

Galingale: *khdenjal*, stalk of the ginger tree, cultivated and wild, from China and the Far East.

Guinea pepper: *gouza sahraouia*, an aphrodisiac from the Ivory Coast.

Nutmeg: *gouza ettiab*, from Sumatra and Java.

Four spices: *nouioura*, pimento from the West Indies. Very different from other pimentos in spite of the name.

Cantharides: *debbal el hand* or 'Spanish fly'.

Cinnamon: *qarfou*, the bark of the tree; from India, the Maldives and Ceylon.

Cyparacée: *tara soudania*, a strong-smelling stalk from Sudan.

Long pepper: *dar felfla*, fruit from the *piper longum*; from India and Malaya.

Cloves: *oud el nouar*, the bud of the clove tree, from Zanzibar.

Curcuma: *orgoub*, yellow root of the ginger tree; from India and other tropical countries.

Ginger: *sknjbir*, the root of the ginger tree.

Orris root: *oud el amber*, found in the high Atlas Mountains.

Black pepper: *elbezar*, fruit of the pepper tree.

Lavender: *kzama*.

Rose-buds: *rous el word*, the rose of Damascus brought from Persia by the Arabs; cultivated in the Dades, Todra and Ferkla valleys.

Ceylon cinnamon: *dar el cini*, the bark of the tree; from tropical Asia.

Ash berries: *lissan ettir*, imported from Europe as an aphrodisiac.

Belladonna berries: *Zbibet el laidour*, dried berries gathered in Chichouen. Very few are needed.

Fennel flowers: *habet el soudane*, seeds cultivated in Morocco.

Gouza el asnab.

White ginger: finer than the grey variety; from Japan.

Asclepiadic fruit: *hilel abachi*.

Cubebe pepper: *kabbaba*, grey scented pepper from Malaya and Borneo.

Monk's pepper: *kheroua*, an aphrodisiac; from Morocco.

OLIVES

The hills surrounding Fez are covered with the grey green of olive trees. There is the festival of the olive harvest and the constant movement of vans on the road. The olive presses are at Bab Guissa, the gate leading north from the city, under the sour black heaps. The rancid smells of the souks. The dripping wooden jugs of the *sahraoui* donkey drivers. Restaurants offer their dishes of olives prepared with lemons. Vendors of fritters with their oily frying-pans. Food with an acid flavour that rasps the throat.

In Fez they have begun to cook with purified olive oil or groundnut oil and seldom use rancid butter. Believe me that nothing is better for preparing a good *tagine* than real olive oil with its fruity taste, which is indispensable in all Moroccan cooking.

When the moment comes for the inhabitants of Fez to take in their annual provisions it is traditional, in order to analyse the quality of the oil they have bought, to use a sample for a *tagine* with cardoons or maybe a nicely browned chicken. Tasting and sipping they will discover the degree of acidity and the olive's subtle perfume.

BLACK OLIVES

The olives, when very ripe black and glistening, are rolled in rock salt in the proportion of two-thirds olives to one-third salt and put into a wicker basket with a heavy flat stone on top; a blackish water will emanate and the salt will penetrate to the fruit. At the end of two months the olives must be washed in clear water and put to dry on the terrace. They keep for a long time packed tightly in jars to avoid all contact with the air, and if dipped in oil may be preserved for many years.

LEMONS PRESERVED IN SALT

Utensils: an absolutely clean jar and a stone.

4 lb ordinary lemons
8 lb small thin or doqq lemons

Put the lemons to soak in water, which must be changed every morning, for five days. At the end of this time divide each lemon in four, taking care that the quarters remain attached. Put a pinch of salt in the middle of each lemon, shut and reshape the fruit. Put the two sorts of lemons into the same jar and place a clean stone on the top. A month later they will be ready. At the end of a few days a juice as thick as honey, but salty, will ooze out and the lemons can be preserved in this indefinitely if kept in a dry place.

You will find that they are used in a number of dishes – meat and vegetable *tagines*, chickens browned in butter. Pregnant women suck them all day long to give them an appetite.

In salads the salty juice is used to advantage instead of vinegar.

BREAD

Every household in Fez kneads the bread necessary for its daily consumption. Very often, Fassis buy the wheat itself, which, picked over, washed and laid to dry on the terrace on a sunny day, is then carried to the mill. When ground it will be divided into four parts: the best flour, soft and pure; the white *lhrama* semolina for *couscous*; the coarse golden semolina from the bran; and finally the bran itself, food for the master's mule. Nothing is wasted.

A solemn religious sentiment accompanies every gesture that touches the grain, the flour and the bread – the respect of a people that has memories of atrocious famines. The gesture of the miserable beggar kissing the piece of bread that he has been given before devouring it. The care of the passer-by in picking up a crust of bread he has found in the road and carefully placing it where it will be seen.

The common oven where everyone's bread is baked and the dough kneaded on every hearth are part of the animation of the street and of the life of each household.

In the street the beggar chants, 'In the name of Allah give me bread,' from door to door. The grating noise of the mill at the edge of the river, songs of the water and the donkey-driver covered with flour. Dressed like women, little girls bring to the oven the round *ksra* balanced on their heads on a board covered with a doubtful looking cloth. On their turbulent heads young boys wear a padded cap on which rests the golden board of baked bread. The luminous oven with its prancing shadows – an emanation of hot bread, a long wait for the crowds of restless squalling brats. Colour … noise … smells.

In the home there is a murmur of invocation to Allah before commencing the almost sacred act of kneading. The soft chatter of the grinding on the sieve accompanied by babbling gossip; the heavy shock of the dough flung on the *gsaa* – gestures learned from childhood which make the girls' arms so shapely.

Time required: from three to five or six hours
according to the season.

Utensil: a *gsaa*.

2 lb sieved flour
Between 1 and 1½ pints water, depending on the
quality of the flour; use tepid water in winter
Yeast
A handful of salt; in Fez, where rock salt is used, it is
best to crush it with your hand
A few spoonfuls of water in the gsaa

Mix the flour and water quickly but stop before it is
a solid mass. Put the yeast in a corner of the *gsaa*
and soften it with a little water.

The yeast will be part of the bread kneaded the
day before, kept in an earthenware pan or in the
flour; in winter it can be kept for several days, but in
summer it turns sour quickly and loses its strength.
If you are not sure of the yeast it is best before using
it to knead it with warm water and a little flour.
Recently yeast from beer has replaced the previous
day's bread, the *ksra* will rise better but the taste will
be less natural.

Mix the yeast with the dough and work hard with
closed fists, kneading with the palm of the hand.
Beat well and add enough water to attain the
consistency of bread dough. Twenty minutes of hard
kneading is necessary for the bread to rise well.

Separate the dough into four parts in the *gsaa*.
Three for the *ksra*, the fourth, about 7 oz, will be for
the yeast for the following day. Roll each of the balls

of dough with a rapid rotating movement in the hollow of your hand so that a cone is formed, which, flattened by light pats becomes a disc about 8 inches in diameter, the *ksra*. Make it rise in the warmth in winter, first put the bread on a board then cover with a cloth and then a woollen blanket.

The *ksra* is ready to put in the oven, when, after having thrust your fingers lightly in the dough, it is sufficiently elastic to return to its original shape.

For feast days mix a teaspoon of sesame or a little aniseed in with the dough. Sprinkle a pinch of sesame on top of the *ksra* before it rises.

The rich consider hard wheat the best for bread-making, while I find tender wheat makes the bread lighter. Poor people, when they cannot afford corn and flour, use barley or maize.

Before sending its bread to the oven each family puts its mark on its loaves – finger prints, a wooden stamp or a simple linear design. These different marks allow everyone to fetch their bread without argument.

SOUPS

HARIRA

It is with this soup that the fast is broken every evening during the month of Ramadan, with which Fassis enjoy appeasing their hunger at the first sound of the cannon at sunset or *moghreb*. These soups are nourishing and very varied, made with dried or fresh vegetables, rice or flour, hot with pepper, rich with mutton, the wings, liver and gizzards of poultry, thickened with yeast or bread, nearly always scented with coriander.

In certain households it is the custom to take *harira* for breakfast during the winter. In the summer a special sort with caraway seeds and ambrosia is served and eaten for dinner by the middle classes of Fez. *Harira* is refreshing, good for the liver and cleanses the stomach, and is most beneficial as a diet after too many good meals.

Go and taste a bowl of one of these soups in any ordinary restaurant in the Fez Djedid, the district to the west of the old town, Boujeloud or Bab Sensla in the town-centre, and you will enjoy the surroundings and I think appreciate the *harira* that will be served to you.

Here is one of the most savoury recipes.

For twelve people.

Time required: two hours.

The neck, gizzard and wings of three or four chickens
1 lb mutton cut into small pieces, or minced and rolled into pellets the size of a marble; beef can also be used
1 finely chopped large onion
5 oz chick-peas soaked in water the day before
A pinch of pepper
A pinch of salt
A small bunch of finely chopped parsley
A pinch of powdered ginger

A pinch of powdered saffron mixed with salt
3 pints water
2 oz butter

Boil for at least two hours, only adding the butter when the water is boiling. When this preparation has been boiling for an hour and a half, put the following into a large pot, adding the rice when the water has come to the boil.

8 pints water
2 oz butter
1 teaspoon pepper
5 oz well washed rice

While the rice is cooking put the following ingredients in a basin.

4 oz bread yeast diluted with 3 pints cold water
A large bunch of coarsely chopped coriander
4 large peeled tomatoes
A handful of salt

When the rice is almost cooked, finish diluting the yeast mixture with the boiling water, put it back on a hot fire, stirring often until it boils again. Let it boil for ten minutes. Add the meat cooked with its liquor.

Serve very hot in china rice bowls or, if they are not available, in pottery or earthenware bowls and drink, inhaling noisily in order to savour all the perfume.

CHORBA

Chorba is a lighter sort of *harira* which takes advantage of the well-flavoured water which has been used for cooking *kefta* or *choua*. This soup can be varied according to your fancy with bits of meat, the remains of chicken and dried vegetables. At the same time that the rice or vermicelli is cooking, prepare a bowl of chopped parsley or coriander to add colour and taste to this soup, which should never be thickened with yeast.

TADEFFI

During the final birth pangs it is customary to prepare a strong broth which the new mother, as soon as she is delivered and has returned to bed, will take after having first swallowed a few raw eggs.

It is composed of chopped garlic, powdered saffron, much pepper, thyme and wild peppermint.

BISTILLA

You have appreciated the subtle richness of this sumptuous dish, brought originally, they say, from Andalusia. You have crunched the crisp pastry, savoured the delicate stuffing; you have thought about learning how to make this dish which is simultaneously sweet and peppery, soft and violent. Alas, you may knead the dough and cook the stuffing, but unless as a little girl you have thrown, like a ball held back by an elastic band, the dab of dough onto the hot metal tray, you will never achieve the perfection of pastry as white, fine and light as tissue paper. If you wish to serve a *bistilla*, get a specialist in this type of pastry to make it for you. If you prepare the stuffing, help with the folding of the sheets of pastry and the final cooking you will not have done too badly!

Jasmina, with infinite patience, has made this difficult dish for us. She arrives at dawn and will not be ready before the evening meal to serve her *chef d'oeuvre*, the most perfect dish in the traditional cooking of Fez, this spicy, frosted golden disc of pastry with its dark exotic stuffing.

For fifteen people.

Utensils: a *gsaa*, a *tobsil dial louarqa*, a *tobsil dettiab* and a *taoua* for cooking the pigeons and another for cooking the eggs.

3 lb 6 oz butter
30 eggs
4 ½ lb flour
10 oz sugar
1 lb 2 oz almonds
1 oz cinnamon
1 oz ginger
A few crushed stalks of Jamaican pimento
A pinch of saffron

9 oz onions
A teaspoon of ras el hanout
A little parsley and coriander

Preparation of the Pastry

Put the flour in the *gsaa*, and little by little sprinkle it with tepid water while kneading well for about fifteen minutes to obtain a dough of the same consistency as that used for making bread. Salt the dough by putting several pinches of salt diluted with water in a corner of the *gsaa*. Knead again, sprinkling with more water in order to get a soft, slightly runny consistency that will spread by itself. Leave it for ten minutes, then continue working, adding water till it reaches the consistency of batter. Beat the paste well to aerate it and make it rise, then leave it for two hours just covered with tepid water.

The Stuffing

While the dough is rising put a pint of water, 1 lb 2 oz of butter, several pinches of salt, the minced onions, the ginger, the *ras el hanout*, the pimento, the finely chopped saffron, a pinch of powdered cinnamon, the coriander and chopped parsely into a *taoua*. Cook the well-cleaned pigeons with their livers and gizzards for three or four hours in this curiously savoury broth.

When the pigeons are perfectly cooked, so that the meat comes easily off the bone, drain them and put them on a dish. Take half the broth in which 20 eggs must be beaten until the mixture is thick like scrambled eggs. Reduce the other half till it becomes a thick gravy. Keep the scrambled eggs and gravy to garnish the inside of the *bistilla*.

The Sheets of Pastry

Beat thoroughly the dough, which should be put aside for two hours, and start to make the sheets of pastry which are cooked one by one. This is the most delicate operation and requires a special skill.

Place the *tobsil dial louarqa* on a very hot large charcoal stove, its edge turned downwards. Dampen your hand and take a small quantity of dough between your fingers, flap it quickly onto the *tobsil*, leaving only a thin transparent patch which will finally form a sheet of pastry about sixteen inches in diameter. The dough, owing to its elasticity and the rapidity of the gesture, will recoil towards your hand the moment it touches the *tobsil*. This movement, which is extremely difficult to get hold of, calls to mind the gesture of the yoyo player, raising and lowering his hand as rapidly as possible. As soon as the bottom of the *tobsil* is covered, lift off the transparent sheet quickly before it turns brown, put it to cool on a cloth and start again as often as is necessary. These very thin sheets are cooked on one side only. One hundred and four will be needed for the amounts given above. Never put the sheets one on top of the other until they are dry.

Garnishing

To prepare for the garnishing of the *bistilla*, sit cross-legged at a round table about 32 inches in diameter. Have the powdered cinnamon and sugar near at hand in separate piles, the almonds, already browned in butter or oil and coarsely chopped, the pigeons cut in small pieces, the scrambled egg sauce and the gravy.

Place on the table twelve sheets of pastry, overlapping in such a way that they hang over the edge, and two sheets in the middle. Stick them together with the ten remaining eggs (yolks and whites). Continue piling the sheets one by one as evenly as possible. Forty sheets are needed for the bottom. Start to garnish within a diameter of 24 inches, sprinkling a mixture of 10 oz sugar, 1 lb 2 oz almonds and 1 oz cinnamon, spread half the scrambled egg mixture and moisten with the sauce from the pigeon broth, now reduced to a thick jelly.

Cover the stuffing with twenty evenly distributed sheets, then place on top the pieces of pigeon, the remains of the scrambled eggs and a little thick gravy. Cover this second garnishing with another twenty sheets. Carefully sticking the sheets together, bring the outer edge of those at the bottom over the top, then put twelve sheets tucked in round the edges to form a perfect round. Finish the *bistilla* by placing the remaining sheets to form its top. Paint the finished dish lightly with yolk of egg. It is important to place the sides of the sheets which have touched the *tobsil dial louarqa*, and are therefore the most cooked, towards the inside in order to avoid the pastry splitting and to achieve perfect cooking.

Cooking

Heat the remains of the butter in the *tobsil dettiab*, with the edge turned upwards. When it is very hot put in the *bistilla*, turn the *tobsil* on the fire to make for oven cooking. Start by cooking the sides of the *bistilla* and then the middle.

When one side is crisp and golden turn carefully by placing a tray under it and sliding it back on to the *tobsil dettiab* to brown the other side, taking care to prick it with a knife to avoid the pastry breaking.

Serve on a china dish, the top sprinkled with soft sugar and powdered cinnamon in a criss-cross pattern.

BROCHETTES

All the various kinds of *brochettes* can be found admirably prepared in any Arab kitchen installed in the street, where, on long iron braziers, six or seven *brochettes* can be cooked at the same time. To appreciate the full savour, take half a *ksra*, open it and slide in the burning hot contents of the *brochette*. Eaten thus, as a sandwich, none of the flavour is lost and the hot and aromatic fat makes the bread delicious.

The quantities given here are for twelve persons, counting one *brochette* per head. The cooking is best done over a charcoal fire.

BOULFAF

Time required: half an hour's preparation; a few minutes' cooking.

1 lb sheep's or calves' liver
A sheep's caul
Salt
Cumin
Hot red pepper

Place the pound of liver on a hot grill, brown it quickly on each side, then cut it into small squares of about an inch. If the sheep's caul is difficult to stretch, soak it in warm water and then cut it into strips. Take a bit of liver, sprinkle it with salt, a pinch of cumin and a suspicion of red pepper. Roll the square in a strip of the sheep's caul. When all the pieces are finished put them on skewers, from six to eight on each, and grill well.

KEBAB

Time required: half an hour's preparation, but take care to marinade the meat for several hours; a few minutes' cooking.

Utensils: a chopper or a mincing machine.

1 lb fillet of beef or mutton cut into pieces of about 1½ inches
½ lb beef or mutton fat cut into smaller pieces
2 medium-sized onions, finely minced
A handful of parsley
Salt
Pepper

Put the pieces of fillet, the fat, the onions, parsley, salt and pepper in a bowl and mix well so that the spices are thoroughly blended and leave to marinade for several hours. Put about ten pieces on each skewer, alternating a piece of fillet with a piece of fat. Grill well on a very hot fire.

KEFTA

Time required: half an hour's preparation and a marinade of several hours; a few minutes' cooking.

1 lb beef; choose fatty meat, if possible, from the ribs
A small bunch of finely chopped coriander
A few coarsely chopped parsley leaves
A blade of sweet marjoram

Salt
A pinch of pepper
A good pinch of hot red soudania pepper
1 heaped teaspoon ras el hanout
1 teaspoon powdered cumin
1 finely chopped onion

Mince the meat very finely, put it in a bowl with the seasoning so that it is very heavily spiced. Mix carefully and leave to marinate. Take a little meat, enough to make a small ball the size of an egg, and pack it tightly around the skewer in the shape of a small sausage. Lay the *keftas* like this in twos and threes. Grill quickly turning them often and serve very hot.

When cooking these different *brochettes*, take care to light the charcoal well in advance and see that it is glowing red before grilling the meat in order to avoid the flavour of smoke affecting the brochettes.

CHOUA

In Fez the *choua* replaces the *mechoui* which is too difficult to prepare in the limited space of a town kitchen. Served as an entrée, it is a simple dish, delicate and easy to digest.

MUTTON CHOUA

For ten people.

Time required: about three hours.

Utensils: two cooking pots, the lower one large and deep and the top one perforated for steaming vegetables or *couscous*, and a pudding-cloth

A quarter of mutton, preferably fatty, weighing
at least 6 ½ lb
Salt
Cumin

Rub the piece of mutton, which will be greatly reduced when steamed, with coarse kitchen salt and wrap it in a pudding-cloth. Fill the bottom cooking pot three-quarters full of water, put the wrapped up meat in the perforated top and bind the two receptacles hermetically to prevent any steam escaping (see p. 83). Steam for about three hours on a hot fire without ever taking off the lid.

This dish is eaten without any other seasoning than salt and powdered cumin, of which everyone takes the amount he wants while eating.

In another recipe the meat is not rubbed with salt but just folded in the cloth. One can also brown the meat when cooked in salted butter.

SHEEP'S HEAD CHOUA

One head will suffice for four people.

Divide the head in two, having first singed and cut with scissors the wool which still remains stuck to the skin. With a chopping knife dig out the horns. Tap and shake this pitiful mask to oust any worms that may still remain in the mouth and nose of the animal. Take out the brains, clean them with ashes, then plenty of water. Cook in the same way as the forequarter of mutton.

The most appreciated part is the eye. You insert a finger delicately in the socket; a quick turn of the nail and the orb will fall out. Extricate it and eat well seasoned with salt and cumin.

CHICKEN CHOUA

Use the same preparation and cooking method as for the forequarter of mutton. The result is delicious.

KEFTA

This is minced meat that you can buy ready-prepared or, even better, having chosen your meat and the right quantity of spices, have it chopped up in front of you by a specialist who possesses a sharp chopping knife, a block cut from an olive tree and solid biceps. Nowadays mincing machines are used to simplify the work, but the *kefta* is not so good. This, I think, is due to the holes in the mincing machine through which the juice runs out, leaving the *kefta* dry. Mutton *kefta* is the most delicate, but beef is also good. The poor use camel's meat and fat and this is what you will generally be offered in the souks.

MUTTON KEFTA

1½ lb mutton cut from the leg
½ lb mutton fat; if sufficient cannot be found, use
beef suet to make up the difference
1 onion
A few leaves of mint
A bunch of parsley
A few leaves of sweet marjoram
1 teaspoon ras el hanout
A few crushed seeds of Jamaican pimento
Salt
1 teaspoon powdered cumin
Hot red soudania pepper to taste

Mince all the ingredients except the *soudania* pepper and cumin which should be added at the end. It is essential to use plenty of the *soudania*, as the delicious peppery *kefta* should almost take your breath away.

Take some minced meat, about the size of a partridge egg, roll it into a ball and use up the rest of the mince in the same way.

Throw the meat balls one by one into a *tagine slaoui* three-quarters full of boiling water and poach them for about a quarter of an hour, taking care that they are not squashed. Turn them so that they are cooked on all sides. Leave them to cool on a board or large dish. The *kefta* balls are now ready to use in all sorts of dishes.

TAGINE WITH KEFTA AND EGGS

For ten people.

Utensils: a *tagine slaoui*.

2 lb 4 oz poached kefta balls
2 oz butter
2 pints of the water in which the kefta balls
were cooked
Salt
Hot red soudania pepper

When the butter and water mixed together are boiling well in the *tagine slaoui* add the salt, *soudania* pepper and the *kefta* balls. Boil on a good fire until the water has nearly evaporated.

Just before serving, break the eggs on top of the balls. They will fry in the sauce, masking the contents of the dish. Serve while the eggs are still crackling.

BRIOUAT

These are 'little letters' stuffed with *kefta*.

Mix the poached *kefta* balls with a few egg yolks to bind and thicken them. Take enough of this stuffing to form a small egg and flatten it; fold in three a sheet of the pastry used in making *bistilla* or *trid*. Place the *kefta* at one end, fold and refold the sheet to form a triangle, or more simply roll the stuffing in the sheet. When all the stuffing is used up heat some butter in a frying pan and when it is very hot put in the *briouat* and fry until they turn golden. While still hot, sprinkle with powdered cinnamon and soft sugar.

RGHAIF

You will see *rghaif* being carried to the common oven like bread. They are about an inch thick, shining with grease and coloured with red pepper. Eaten hot, they are served with tea for breakfast.

To make the stuffing you will need:

> *1 lb minced mutton or beef fat*

Hot and sweet red pepper to taste
1 teaspoon powdered cumin
1 finely chopped onion
Parsley

Cook all the ingredients slightly so that the fat begins to melt.

The Pastry

In the *gsaa* mix some flour and water into a dough which is softer than bread dough but less liquid than that used for fritters. Add a little salt. Knead continuously for a good half hour until the dough becomes elastic. Use at once.

Lightly butter or oil the *gsaa*, take a handful of dough about the size of an egg, spread it on the *gsaa*, stretching and flattening it with your fingertips dipped in the melted fat. To obtain perfect pastry each sheet should be about the thickness of a sheet of paper between 8 and 16 inches long.

Garnishing and Folding

While the sheet of pastry is still on the *gsaa*, sprinkle a tablespoon of stuffing on a third of it. Fold in three and roll. Replace this cylinder on end in the *gsaa*, supporting it with one hand, flatten it with the other, then tap it with all the fingers to shape it into a round of about 18 inches in diameter. While doing this don't forget to dip your fingers into the fat frequently. The pastry can be folded the same way without any stuffing.

Cook in the oven or fry in an earthenware pan rubbed with oil and onion.

TRID

Known in Fez as the poor man's *bistilla*, *trid* is said to have been the favourite food of the prophet Mohammed.

Much skill is required to make *trid*, as well as a

turn of the hand which is not easily acquired. You can, however, buy them ready-made in all the restaurants of Boujeloud and they are excellent.

The dough is the same as that used for *rghaif*. Knead it for a good half hour until it is exceedingly elastic, then put the dough to soak in oil in an earthenware bowl. The sheet of pastry is not cooked on a stove but on the *gdra del trid*. With well-oiled hands take a ball of dough the size of an egg, stretch it quickly in the *gsaa*. The sheet will cook quickly, remaining soft, white and transparent. When cool pile up on a round dish.

SNAILS

In Morocco snails are called by the amusing name of *boubbouches*; they are not large and grey like the well-known ones from Burgundy, but of medium size, white encircled with black. You will savour them served hot or cold in pottery bowls, swimming in the fierce soup made from the liquor in which they have been cooked and which is supposed to whet the appetite, purify the blood and cure stomach-ache. To extract them use a simple wild acacia thorn.

For ten pounds of snails.

A large pinch of green aniseed
A large pinch of caraway seed
2 or 3 pieces of liquorice root
A tablespoonful of thyme
A small handful of green tea
A sprig of sage
A small bunch of mint
The rind of a bitter orange
A sprig of sweet marjoram
A pinch of hot red soudania pepper
A few crushed seeds of gum mastic
Salt to taste

Leave the snails to fast for a few days in an airy receptacle in a dry place in the open air. Before cooking, wash them seven times – three times in fresh water, once stirred round with a large quantity of salt, then rinse again three times in fresh water and finally put them to drain.

Heat enough water in a cooking pot to cover the snails. As soon as the water boils put in the spices, herbs and salt, stir for a few minutes, then throw in the snails and cook for at least two hours with the lid on. Leave the *boubbouches* to cool in this liquid and reheat just before serving. The broth can be drunk alone or while eating the snails, hot or cold, but, in my opinion, it is most efficacious taken boiling hot and has more flavour. This medicinal appetizer can be kept two or three days.

COUSCOUS

This is the Moroccan national dish. It will be served to you at the end of a copious meal by your host anxious to saturate your already failing appetite and you will be incapable of tasting more than one or two mouthfuls. On the other hand, if invited informally by friends and sitting round the table you are given *couscous*, you can, with impunity, stuff yourself with this semolina, each grain separated from the other, so light, smooth and scented, and digested with incredible ease. You must take in your right hand a chick-pea or a raisin with a handful of semolina, press and shape it carefully to form a small ball and and an expert twist of the thumb should carry it to your mouth. As you will probably only succeed in besmearing yourself with grease it is better to ask for a spoon. But learn to appreciate the contrast between the softness of the raisins and the sharp burning of the peppery semolina.

The Grain

To prepare fine and regular grain needs much patience and a skill which can only be acquired after long practice.

In former times each family rolled its own grain; now you can find excellent packets of *couscous* in the shops and so the work is simplified – only make sure that they are fresh.

For twenty people.

Time required: four hours.

Utensils: a *kskas* and its *tanjra* in copper or in glazed earthenware. In the east near the high tablelands where esparto grass grows, the *kskas* is a basket made from the grass, but whatever the material the top part must fit exactly into the cooking pot. A *gsaa* and a large, round Fez earthenware serving dish.

4 lb 8 oz rolled semolina
2 lb 4 oz of neck, shoulder or cutlets of mutton
1 lb 2 oz beef (optional)
*1 chicken and the gizzards of other poultry if
possible*
1 lb 2 oz onions

5 oz chick-peas cooked the day before
A bunch of turnips
1 lb 2 oz carrots
1 lb 2 oz marrow
2 handfuls of broad beans (in season)
3 tomatoes
1 cabbage heart
A few sprigs of parsley
A bunch of finely chopped coriander
9 oz raisins
A good pinch of powdered saffron
11 oz butter
A ladle of olive oil
½ teaspoon pepper
A handful of salt
A suspicion of hot red soudania pepper
6 pints water for the broth and what is needed for
moistening the couscous

Put into the cooking pot six pints of water, the mutton, the whole chicken rubbed with pepper and saffron, the chopped onions, pepper, chick-peas, carrots, salt, saffron, olive oil and 3 oz butter for the broth. Boil for at least an hour.

Spread out on the *kskas* a layer of semolina about 1½ inches deep. Moisten slightly, shake the grains to let in the air and make them swell better. Put the *kskas* on top of the pot where the broth is cooking, bind a cloth dipped in flour and water round where the two pots meet so that the steam cannot escape except through the holes where the semolina is cooking, add the rest of the *couscous* and cook for three-quarters of an hour.

For this dish one can use mutton only, or replace the mutton by two chickens or a turkey. In certain households they add beef, the mixture giving a more traditional flavour.

Take off the *kskas* without disturbing the semolina. Now wet it thoroughly with cold water and leave to drain, then stir round the bottom lightly with the handle of a wooden spoon.

Now add the turnips, coriander, parsley, marrow, broad beans, tomatoes and cabbage to the broth.

Returning to the semolina, put a good teaspoonful of salt dissolved in about half a pint of water in the *gsaa*. Throw in the *couscous*, stirring and separating the grains so that the salt penetrates everywhere, sprinkle with cold water, lifting and letting the air in lightly with your hands to make the *couscous* swell. Repeat until the semolina is saturated with water and leave it on one side to cool in the *gsaa*. Throw the raisins into the broth.

When the *couscous* is almost cold, divide it into four or five parts. Now proceed with the second cooking of the semolina, similar to the first, but, instead of dividing the *couscous* in two parts, return it to the *kskas* in four or five separate layers, taking care not to add the next layer until the steam has come well through the one before. Cook for about half an hour.

Reduce the broth on a hot fire.

Put the *couscous* on the serving dish, separating the grains with the tips of your fingers and working in the rest of the butter little by little.

Arrange the *couscous* in a high cone-shaped mass, then put the meat and chicken covered with vegetables in the middle and pour the broth over the whole dish.

In European homes the semolina is usually served separately, the meat on another dish and the broth and vegetables in a tureen.

To add to the hot spicy flavour of this dish prepare in a sauceboat two glasses of broth with a pinch of red *soudania* pepper; the guests can then help themselves to this hot sauce according to their taste.

CHARIYA

In the *gsaa* make a dough of the same consistency as for bread, with flour, salt and water. Lay aside for several hours. Then take a small pellet of dough, roll it between the thumb and forefinger or in the palm of the hand. It becomes round in the centre, then at the ends, less than half an inch thick. Use up all the dough in the same way. Put it to dry on a cloth in the sun. *Chariya* can be kept for some time in a tin.

It is used in *harira*, like vermicelli in soup, and steamed in salted water in the *couscous* pot and served after rolling in butter.

It is eaten garnished with sugar and powdered cinnamon, with a bowl of cold milk for each person to drink. Place a saucer of sugar and powder-red cinnamon in front of each guest.

Salads

Served during the meal, these refreshing salads, varied in colour and scent, will make you forget the heaviness of the preceding dish and whet your appetite for the *tagines* to follow.

Radish Salad

Grate several long red-skinned radishes which have been washed but not peeled. Sprinkle heavily with sugar, mix in a peeled orange cut into small pieces, add lemon juice and a pinch of salt.

Parsley Salad

Mix together in a dish a large bunch of chopped parsley, a well-minced fresh onion and the pulp of a large lemon cut into small pieces; sprinkle the juice of a lemon on this mixture and add a pinch of salt.

Orange Salad

Peel a few oranges and cut them into large pieces, taking out the pips, add a few spoonfuls of orange flower water, stir, then sprinkle lightly with powdered cinnamon. A very soothing salad.

LETTUCE HEARTS

A well-chopped heart of a tender lettuce, a pinch of salt, a lot of pepper, oil, vinegar, a pinch of cinnamon ... and to add to the taste do not hesitate to sprinkle well with sugar.

COS LETTUCE SALAD

A fine cos lettuce, finely chopped, sprinkled with the juice of two oranges, a pinch of salt and a good deal of pepper. A curious and very refreshing mixture.

APPLE, TOMATO AND PIMENTO SALAD

Boil for twenty minutes garlic, chopped onion, red pepper, chopped parsley, oil and peeled and seeded tomatoes cut into small pieces. Drain and then add hot and sweet peppers which you have already grilled on charcoal, skinned, seeded and cut up. Finally, add the apples, cut in half, cored but not peeled. Add *soudania* to taste. Eat cold.

CUCUMBER SALAD

Grate the cucumbers. Season with vinegar, chopped thyme, caraway seeds, salt and sugar. If you don't like sugar use a little oil. In all salads lemon can replace vinegar.

EGGS

Street sellers offer shelled hard-boiled eggs garnished with a pinch of salt and cumin.

In Fez eggs are fried in oil or butter with a little salt, red pepper and cumin.

Eggs are served round many *tagines* and to thicken the stuffing of the *bistilla*. You will find them used in many of the recipes in this book.

LBEN

'*Lben! ... Lben!*' The street cry is heard in Fez as soon as the fine weather arrives. Drunk by rich and poor, city dweller and *fellah*, it is offered in the shops to all who pass by. May you one day know the joy of quenching your thirst with this slightly acidic whey, drunk in the pale shadow of an olive tree after a long excursion on a hot day in June. In a tent the goatskin has been kept, prepared and sewn. In the spring the hair *chkoua* or goatskin bottle is ready to receive the milk which is curdled naturally in a *khabia* that is never rinsed. The branch of the tree – the piece of wood where the goatskin bottle will hang from *doum* ropes – is waiting, marked by the previous year's notches.

Patiently, the woman, a song on her lips, will sway backwards and forwards with the *chkoua* till a characteristic sound of plashing is heard. This means that the molecules of fat have separated from the liquid. After having poured the *lben* into a jar, the open *chkoua* will be washed. The yellow grains floating on the top of the jar will be collected and patted together, but not kneaded, and served for breakfast or lunch with hot cakes. All day long the family and visitors will find this pure and refreshing drink ready to hand whenever they want it. Don't forget to add two pints of water, tepid in spring, cold in summer, to the ten pints of curdled milk in the *chkoua* or in the jar to aid the operation.

BUTTER

There are two kinds of butter, the fresh *zebda* and the melted *smen*.

In Arab countries they make their butter by skimming it off the top of the curdled milk *lben* in the way described on p. 91. It is therefore difficult to produce fresh-tasting butter, and it is easy to understand that if the goatskin churn is not kept very clean, or if the curds have been too long in the unwashed *khabia*, the butter obtained will be sour and often have a mouldy smell. The butter floats on the top of the *lben* jar in round clots, unkneaded and swollen with whey. It will be eaten with hot cakes and certain pastries, put in the semolina of the *couscous*, used for greasing the *kdra* and browning the *bistilla*. In the spring when it is most plentiful Fassis melt and store it for the winter.

In the country butter is made from ewe's milk, but when melted it is not as strong as cow's milk and not as widely appreciated.

SMEN

When melted, the butter is skimmed during the boiling, which lasts about a quarter of an hour, and then strained through a fine cloth into the *khabia* where it is kept. Salt it lightly before it curdles, stirring with a wooden spoon. A white deposit remains at the bottom of the cooking-pan. Use a ladle for pouring the butter.

It is this *smen* which, if not carefully made, gives that rancid flavour to the sauces which, however, is found more and more rarely in cooked dishes nowadays.

The older the *smen*, the stronger it becomes and the less is needed. To keep it many years is a sign of abundance and riches and only very wealthy families can afford this luxury. If it is brought out on a special occasion at a house where you are a guest, this is an honour and you must taste it.

FISH

SHAD

The shad, in spawn, come up the River Sebou towards the end of December. For several months this fish, sold in pairs, fleshy and full of bones, provides a great treat for the Fassi.

FRIED SHAD

For twelve people.

Time required: four hours, as the fish must be left to marinade several hours before frying.

Utensils: a hollow dish and a frying pan or *mqla*.

A fine shad
A bunch of coriander
A dozen cloves of garlic
A good handful of salt
2 lemons
1 tablespoon sweet red pepper
A pinch of hot red pepper
1 tablespoon powdered cumin

Gut the shad, taking care to reserve the hard or soft roes, which are much appreciated. Throw away the head and tail. Rinse the fish several times in salt water. Divide it first into two lengthwise, then cut up into pieces and wash again carefully. In a large hollow dish put the salt, finely chopped garlic and coriander together with the two peppers and the cumin. Dilute with the juice of two lemons. This preparation is not only intended to flavour the shad but has also, they say, the power of melting the bones.

Put the pieces of fish and the roes in this marinade and let them soak for several hours. Drain well, then roll in flour and throw them into boiling fat. Cook till they are nicely browned.

In Fez fried shad are generally eaten cold, and thus found easier to digest, but they are also excellent hot, and the roes, hard or soft, are offered to the guest as a special treat and sign of honour.

SHAD WITH STUFFED DATES

For twelve persons.

Time required: four hours' preparation and cooking.

Utensils: a fire-proof dish – a large *tagine slaoui* will do very well.

A fine large shad
1 lb dates
3 oz almonds
3 oz rice or semolina
1 tablespoon sugar
½ teaspoon powdered ginger
½ teaspoon powdered cinnamon
3 oz of butter
A good deal of pepper
A very small pinch of salt
Half an onion

Gut the shad and wash in salt water.

Wash and stone the heavy black dates from the Tafilalet oasis.

Prepare the stuffing, composed of the boiled or steamed rice mixed, when cold, with the chopped almonds, sugar, a little butter, a pinch of pepper and ginger. Stuff the dates with this preparation.

Fill the fish with the stuffed dates, sew up the belly carefully.

Lay the shad on a fire-proof dish (in which it will also be served) with the remains of the butter, a soup ladle of water, plenty of pepper and very little salt, a pinch of ginger and the finely chopped onion.

Cook slowly in the oven. When done undo the belly, take out the dates and put them round the dish.

Dust with cinnamon and put back in the oven to brown. When the water has evaporated, the juice caramelised and the skin is crisp and golden, the dates soft and unctuous, the shad is ready to serve.

This recipe, which may seem curious to you, is one of the most marvellous to be found in Fassi cooking. The dates can be replaced by prunes, and other large fish such as carp can be cooked in the same way.

TAGINES

To make these exotic stews, varied in flavour, spiced and sweet, typical of the cooking of Fez, you will need a *taoua*, the high round copper-plated stew pan, and the round dish of glazed earthenware with a pointed lid, the *tagine slaoui* that will enable you to serve your stews piping hot. In the *tagine slaoui* the meat will be covered with the garnish, and the water having evaporated, the sauce will be very thick. The dish can be kept hot on a slow fire and when almost ready for serving placed in a copper pan of boiling water enclosed in the *tbiqa*, the stiff round basket with a cone-shaped cover. The shape and gay colours of the *tbiqa* arranged before the meal in front of the open door of the reception room lend the atmosphere of a Chinese feast to the patio.

The great principle of the *tagine*, the secret of the meat which is always tender, is to simmer it for many hours, according to the recipe in a seasoned and fragrant *court bouillon*, the oil or butter mingling with the meat juices to form a soft velvety sauce which exudes a strange perfume.

You can use chickens, pigeons, turkey, mutton, or, as a last resort, beef. I have also eaten camel *tagine*, as this meat replaces beef for the poor and has a somewhat similar flavour.

Since the war Fassis have found it difficult to procure the butter necessary for making the *smen* in the spring to be used during the year. Because of the price they have now learned to use the more economical groundnut oil, which although it does not have the subtle flavour of the butter, has the advantage of being tasteless. The *kdra* or the *tagine mahammer* can be cooked in this oil alone, or better still mixed with butter. In the past groundnut oil was unknown and the *tagines* in Fez were always cooked in olive oil or *smen*.

The proportions of these dishes are given for a normal appetite but, when wishing to honour their guests, Fassis insist that the *tagine slaoui* should contain at least four medium or three large chickens, and other meats and vegetables in the same proportions.

Above all, never forget that a good *tagine* should be eaten so hot that you will probably burn your fingers.

CHICKEN

'In the name of Allah.' The sacrificer pronounces the consecrated formula at the same time as slaughtering the bird. With ruffled feathers and its eyes full of terror, the fowl is thrown into the street in its death throes. In spurting drops, life drains from the bird in a viscous pool.

The little *mtallma* or servant is waiting. She seizes the dead bird, plunges it into boiling water, plucks and draws it, washes it several times in cold water. In a few minutes nothing is left of the multi-coloured bird but a bluish shape, its neck and wings cut off, ready to undergo all the various ways of cooking which are given in the following recipes.

Arriving by bus, the chickens, crammed together by the dozen in wicker baskets, are taken off screeching and attached in bunches to a donkey's back. With heads swaying about and beaks open, they descend into the *medina*.

CHICKEN WITH OLIVES AND LEMONS

Utensils: a *taoua* and a *tagine slaoui*.

Time required: three hours.

1 chicken
1 finely chopped onion
1 clove of garlic
A bunch of finely chopped coriander and parsley
A bunch of saffron finely pounded with salt
½ teaspoon pepper
A ladle of olive oil
7 oz olives
3 preserved lemons

Put the onion, garlic, coriander, parsley, saffron and pepper in the *taoua*. Lay the trussed chicken on top, half cover it in water, add salt, cover it and bring to the boil, then add the olive oil. During the cooking take care to turn the chicken now and again. When the flesh is soft and comes off the bone easily, take out the chicken and reduce the sauce until the water has completely evaporated. Put the chicken back in the *taoua*, leave to simmer for a few minutes and serve very hot in the *tagine slaoui*. Garnish with the olives, lemons, liver and gizzard and pour the meat juice over the entire dish.

A shoulder of mutton can be used instead of a chicken for this *tagine*.

STUFFED CHICKEN

CHICKEN STUFFED WITH ALMONDS, SEMOLINA AND RAISINS

For four people.

Time required: four hours for the preparation and cooking.

Utensils: a stewing pan and a *tagine slaoui*.

1 large chicken

Having slaughtered, plucked, drawn and washed the chicken according to the *caïda* or tradition, fill its cavity with a stuffing composed of:

2 ½ oz coarsely chopped almonds
3 ½ oz steamed couscous semolina
A small piece of butter the size of a walnut added to the semolina
5 oz cleaned and chopped raisins
1 small teaspoon powdered ras el hanout

Add salt and mix all the ingredients well together till the stuffing is smooth, then fill the chicken, truss and sew up the belly carefully.

Then put the following ingredients in a stewing pan:

> *A pinch of powdered ginger*
> *1 chopped onion*
> *1 teaspoon salt*
> *A pinch of saffron pounded with salt*

Lay the chicken in the pan, half cover with water and place on a quick fire. When the water boils add 3 oz butter. Boil quickly until the meat comes easily off the bone – for about two hours.

The water having evaporated, brown the chicken in the butter. Serve in a *tagine slaoui*.

The way to eat this dish is first to rub the chicken with a bit of bread, then dip the bread in the sauce round the bottom of the dish and enjoy this savoury morsel. Take the boiling hot meal delicately with the tips of your fingers, break the breast bone and attack the stuffing, golden and sweet with a flavour which will surprise and astonish the most jaded palate.

Chicken stuffed with Almonds, Semolina, Raisins and Honey

The stuffing is slightly different from the previous recipe. The almonds are fried in butter before being chopped, the raisins seeded and left whole, the ginger replaced by a large pinch of *ras el hanout*, powdered cinnamon and very little pepper, saffron, butter and salt; finally, two good spoonfuls of honey are added.

Stuff the chicken, sew up the belly and truss. In the liquor in which the chicken is cooked put a large pinch of pepper, ginger, cinnamon, an onion, a little oil or butter, and when it is just ready to serve add a little honey to taste. Heat again for a few minutes.

Arrange the chicken in the *tagine slaoui*, garnish with the gizzard and liver cut into little pieces. The strong dose of pepper will bring out the sweetness of the honey and prevent the dish from being sickly.

Mutton can be cooked in the same way, as can turkey using three times the quantity of stuffing.

MUTTON

The sheep is the animal whose meat serves as a basis for the Moslem's diet.

When, on the day of Eid el Kebir, the festival marking Abraham's sacrifice, a sheep is slaughtered in every household, the head, trotters, offal, every part of the animal is put to some use. There will be feasting for several days. The meat that cannot be consumed will be preserved, dried in the sun and covered with fat. The bones and gristle are used for the *mrouzia*. As well as dishes where only mutton is used, all *tagines* can be made with this meat, which is particularly good in Morocco, above all in the spring when the animal is fat.

MUTTON STUFFED WITH ALMONDS, SEMOLINA AND RAISINS

For the stuffing, see the different chicken recipes in the previous chapter.

Take a forequarter of mutton, shoulder and cutlets, and introduce the stuffing by gently pulling away the skin and sliding it with care between the skin and the meat and bone under the shoulder. Sew

back, tie up with string and brown like the chicken. Preparing this dish is a long and meticulous task, but the result is delicious.

GRILLED SHEEP'S HEAD

If you pass by the Bab Sensla in the town-centre, you will notice round bake houses made of limestone and earth. Shut up inside them are dozens of sheep's heads, cleaned in salt water, sheared and singed, split in half with an axe as far as the neck which still unites the two parts when the brain has been taken out.

The oven is heated in the evening, the opening blocked by a mess of mud and grass, and the heads are left to cook till the next morning, a thick layer of grass alternating with a row of heads.

At dawn they will be brought out one by one as they are asked, for boiling hot, stewed, smoked and slightly grilled. The bloated skin comes away easily, and you will find that the cheeks and tongue, eaten hot with just salt and cumin, have a most delicate flavour.

Hergma

TAGINE OF SHEEP'S TROTTERS

For ten people.

Time required: four hours for preparation and cooking.

15 sheep's trotters
1 lb 2 oz chick-peas
10 oz wheat or rice
1 teaspoon powdered ginger
1 teaspoon sweet red pepper
A pinch of hot red soudania pepper
A ladle of olive oil
2 finely chopped onions

To clean the trotters, grill them and scrape off the outside rind and cut out the nails. Divide them into three.

Wash the meat thoroughly and crush it roughly with the pestle and mortar, rubbing off as much tegument as possible between your hands.

Put the oil, spices, onions, salt, sheep's trotters, the chick-peas soaked the day before and skinned and the crushed wheat in a stew pan. Cover with water. Cook for a long time on a slow fire.

The wheat can be replaced by boiled or steamed rice which has been left to cool and then reheated.

Arrange in a *tagine slaoui*.

MROUZIA

This dish of Eid el Kebir is preserved until the festival of the prophet Mohammed's birthday or the Moslem new year. The meat conserve is a magnificent dark amber colour and is not sickly thanks to the spices which give it a surprising relish. To keep *mrouzia*, put it in a little earthenware jar, the meat first and the raisins and almonds on top, and cover with the sauce.

For twenty people.

Time required: five to six hours.

11 ¼ lb mutton; the bones of the leg, the joints and the gristle are generally used, but do not fear to use good legs of mutton as your guests will be all the better fed
5 lb 10 oz raisins
1 lb 2 oz almonds
1 pint olive oil
1 lb 2 oz butter
3 lb 2 oz honey
A big pinch of saffron pounded with salt
2 finely chopped large onions
1 tablespoon pounded ras el hanout
Salt

In a stewpan, at the bottom of which a plate should be put upside down to prevent the meat from sticking, put three pints of water, the oil, butter, onions, salt, *ras el hanout*, saffron and the meat. Put on the lid and boil rapidly for three hours. Add the honey and when the mixture returns to the boil turn down the fire and leave it to simmer gently without stirring. Add the raisins, which should be topped and tailed and washed. Take the pan off the fire when the water has completely evaporated.

Arrange the meat with the bones in a *tagine slaoui*, then put the raisins on top and cover with the peeled almonds browned in butter, pouring the thick juice over the whole dish.

OTHER MEATS

PIGEON

Fassis are partial to this rather tasteless bird which is used in the delicate stuffing of the *bistilla*, in *tagines* with spring vegetables and fruit instead of mutton or chicken. It is also considered a great treat in *couscous*.

GAME

Hare is seldom served in Fez. First the hunter or trapper must catch it alive and slaughter it according to religious rites. It will then be cooked with many spices in the same way as *tagine mahammer* without vegetables or *tagine mqalli*. These *tagines* prepared with hare should always have raisins and a good spoonful of *ras el hanout*.

Partridge cooked like chicken, browned or fried, is found on the Fassi dining-table even less often than hare.

Gazelle and moufflon (wild sheep) are only eaten in the country, as is the hedgehog, which is much appreciated by the countryman.

Whatever way game is cooked, a good pinch of *ras el hanout* is always added.

Turkey

In Fassi kitchens, turkey is prepared in the same way as chicken. Turkey is always served for a meal of any importance, a fine bird being a pleasure to the eye as well as to the taste-buds.

Rabbit

Rabbit is cooked like a *tagine mahammer* with *ras el hanout*. Raisins and grilled almonds are added a few minutes before serving.

Beef

This meat, less appreciated in Fez than mutton, can be cooked in the same way in *tagines*, in *couscous*, *hergma* and *kefta*.

Goat

This animal with its voracious appetite is partly responsible for the disappearance of the Moroccan forest and unprotected trees in the gardens round Fez. It is the poor man's meat; tougher, stronger-smelling and cheaper, it can be used in the same way as mutton.

CAMEL

With a conceited, contradictory and unpleasant air, the camel arrives in convoys at souk el Khemis, the Thursday market. He occupies an important place in the market, blocks the streets of the *medina* on his way down to the slaughter-house and finishes up on the butcher's stall cut up in unappetising violet coloured pieces destined as minced meat for *kefta*. The white and sickly fat from the hump, cut out in huge thick petals, decorates the stall and will be bought to make the *khli* (preserved meat) of mutton, beef or camel.

Less expensive, it can be cooked in the same way as beef, on a day when there is nothing else to be had, especially if the meat comes from a young camel.

FRIED, BROWNED AND MARINADED MEATS

Certain dishes – *el lham el mqalli* and *el lham el mchermel* – used to be cooked only in olive oil, while others – *kdras* and *el lham el mahammer* – were always cooked in *smen*. Increase the quantity of fat when the meat is lean and reduce it when the meat is very fat. Nowadays groundnut oil or fresh butter can also be used.

El Lham el Mqalli
MUTTON MQALLI

The principal spices used in this dish are ginger and saffron. It can be garnished, served in the *tagine slaoui* with lemons and olives. Finely chopped onions bring out the taste of the meat. A touch of garlic and a bunch of coriander add a subtle flavour.

For ten people.

Time required: three hours.

Utensils: a *taoua* for cooking and a *tagine slaoui* for serving.

4 lb shoulder and cutlets of mutton
½ pint olive oil
A good pinch of powdered ginger
A pinch of saffron powdered with salt
2 finely chopped large onions
A bunch of coriander removed before serving
2 crushed cloves of garlic
½ lb olives
6 preserved lemons cut in quarters
Salt to taste

Put oil, ginger, saffron and salt in the *taoua*, dilute with half a pint of water poured on little by little. Cut the meat in pieces and roll in this mixture. Add sufficient water almost to cover the meat. Put in the onions and coriander. Cook on a quick fire. Take out the meat when it is cooked, let the sauce reduce until it is thick and oily. Put the meat back with the olives and lemons, leave to simmer for a few minutes and serve very hot in the *tagine slaoui*, with the olives and lemons on the top and the sauce poured over the whole dish.

Chicken and turkey can be cooked in the same way.

El Lham el Mahammer
BRAISED MEAT

Coloured with red pepper, perfumed with ginger, browned in melted butter, prepared with mutton, chicken or even a turkey. To vary the following recipe, potatoes fried in butter may be added, or half a pound of peeled almonds fried in butter. Sometimes, just before serving, the dish is garnished with eggs fried in butter.

For ten people.

Time required: four hours.

Utentils: a *taoua*, a *mqla* and a *tagine slaoui*.

4 ½ lb shoulder and cutlets of mutton cut into three
or four pieces
A large pinch of powdered ginger
2 large pinches of sweet red pepper
2 pinches of powdered saffron
2 large pinches of powdered cumin
2 large onions
3 crushed cloves of garlic
1 lb 2 oz butter
¼ pint olive oil
Salt to taste

Choose a fat piece of mutton, shoulder and cutlets. Divide into three or four pieces. Pound the saffron with a little salt, dilute with a few tablespoons of water and rub the mutton well with this golden perfume.

Put the mutton into the *taoua*, add 2 oz of butter, a third of the oil, the red pepper, garlic, onions, ginger, cumin, salt and enough water to half cover the meat. Take out the meat when it is well cooked. Reduce the sauce.

Heat the rest of the butter and oil in the *mqla*,

throw in the pieces of drained and cold meat. Brown well on both sides. Serve in the *tagine slaoui* with both cooking liquors poured over it.

El Lham el Mchermel
MARINADED MEAT

The meat, heavily seasoned and cut into large pieces, is put to marinade for two to three hours.

For ten people.

Time required: three hours.

Utensils: a *taoua* and a *tagine slaoui* for serving.

4 ½ lb shoulder and cutlets of mutton
1 lb 2 oz onions
3 finely chopped cloves of garlic
½ pint olive oil
2 large pinches of ginger
A few crushed cumin seeds
A pinch of sweet red pepper
A small piece of cinnamon stick
A large pinch of pepper
A bunch of chopped parsley
A handful of chopped coriander
The juice of a large lemon
3 or 4 preserved lemons
½ lb olives

Put garlic, saffron, red pepper, cumin and pepper in a dish and rub the meat well with these spices. Leave to macerate in a *taoua* for two or three hours, adding the cinnamon stick in a little cold water. Then bring to the boil and add the oil; when the meat comes easily off the bone it is cooked. Leave it aside on a dish.

Simmer the onions, parsley and coriander in the spicy liquor in the *taoua* till it becomes a thick golden cream in which the pieces of meat are reheated, first one third, another third ten minutes later and the rest after fifteen minutes. Bring to the boil and cook for a quarter of an hour.

Arrange and keep hot in the *tagine slaoui*, the meat covered by the purée of onions. Squeeze lemon juice over the dish before serving and decorate with lemons and olives.

This can be served without the lemons and olives, but do not forget the lemon juice.

Qamama Tagines

These *tagines* made with onions are among the best, but their preparation is rather lengthy. You will be praised by all when you put this dish on the table, crisp and golden, caramelised with honey or pungent with lemon.

Qamama Tagine with Honey

For ten people.

Time required: four hours.

Utensils: a *taoua* and a *tagine slaoui*.

4 ½ lb mutton cut into pieces of about 2 oz
One large piece of cinnamon
½ teaspoon powdered ginger
A large pinch of powdered saffron
2 lb 4 oz onions
1 lb honey
A small pinch of salt

Cook the pieces of meat in the *court bouillon* of spices, saffron, ginger, cinnamon, four tablespoons of honey and enough water to half cover the meat. When the meat is half-cooked and the liquid reduced by three-quarters, take a *tagine slaoui* and arrange in it the pieces of meat with the onions piled on top, pour over the liquid from the stew, cover with the pointed lid that has a hole pierced in the top, cook in a hot oven for at least an hour till the onions are well browned and the water evaporated.

Take the *tagine* out of the oven, pour over it the rest of the honey, strained and heated, put back in the oven for twenty minutes. Perfumed and cooked to bursting point, these onions should melt in the mouth.

QAMAMA TAGINE WITH LEMON

For ten people.

Time required: four hours.

Utensils: a *taoua* and a *tagine slaoui*.

4 ½ lb mutton cut into pieces
2 lb 4 oz onions
¼ teaspoon powdered red pepper
½ teaspoon cumin
¼ teaspoon ginger
A pinch of powdered saffron
2 chopped cloves of garlic
A bunch of coriander
3 lemons

Cook the meat, half-covered with water in the *taoua*

with the red pepper, cumin, ginger, saffron, garlic, one chopped onion, the bunch of coriander and the juice of one lemon. When the meat is cooked take it out of the *taoua* and put in the rest of the chopped onion; cover until it is completely cooked. Arrange the pieces of meat in the *tagine slaoui*, add the onions reduced to a purée and pour over the juice of two lemons. Put to brown in a hot oven.

Two chickens cut up in pieces can be used instead of mutton.

TFAIA TAGINE

This dish comes, they say, from Andalusia and can be made with mutton, beef or chicken. It is best cooked with *smen*, but good olive oil or groundnut oil can also be used.

For ten people.

Time required: three hours.

Utensils: a *taoua* and a *tagine slaoui*.

4 ½ lb mutton cut into large pieces from the shoulder and cutlets
½ teaspoon powdered ginger
A pinch of saffron pounded with salt
10 oz smen
1 or 2 cloves of garlic
A bunch of coriander
1 lb 2 oz almonds browned in butter
6 hard-boiled eggs

Prepare and cook the same way as *tagine mqalli* (see p.116). When the eggs are hard-boiled peel them. Dilute a pinch of saffron in a little water and roll the eggs in the liquid, heated so that the yellow penetrates and colours the white eggs.

Serve boiling hot in a *tagine slaoui*, the meat garnished with the almonds browned in butter and the eggs divided in two lengthwise.

Kdras

Kdras are *tagines* cooked in *smen*. You can use fresh butter or mix butter and oil half-and-half, but to keep to tradition only *smen* should be used – the more rancid it is, the less you need! A *kdra* is cooked in the same way as a *tagine*, but ginger is never used as in the former. Plenty of onions are used, well cooked until they form a purée. The *kdra* with dried vegetables is better made with chicken and a bunch of parsley, leaving mutton and beef to be cooked with fresh vegetables and coriander.

Kdra with almonds and chick-peas

For ten people.

Time required: four hours.

Utensils: a *taoua* and a *tagine slaoui*.

*2 chickens cut in half or 4 ½ lb shoulder
and cutlets of mutton
1 lb 2 oz chick-peas soaked the day before
10 oz almonds
2 lb 4 oz onions
A piece of cinnamon stick
A pinch of saffron pounded with salt
1 teaspoon ground pepper
7 oz butter*

A bunch of chopped parsley
The juice of a large lemon

Put the salt and saffron, pepper, cinnamon, a chopped onion, chick-peas and the meat in the *taoua*, cover with water and cook for about two hours. Then add the almonds. After they have cooked for half an hour take them out and put in the rest of the finely chopped onion and the parsley. Cook till the onions are quite soft and form a purée and the liquid is very much reduced.

Arrange in the *tagine slaoui* with the chick-peas, the almonds and the sauce on top of the onions and meat. Serve very hot with the juice of a lemon added at the last minute.

These *kdras* can be made in the same way with potatoes, turnips or courgettes instead of almonds and chick-peas, and a bouquet of coriander replacing the parsley.

Spring tagines

Tagine with wild artichoke hearts

Towards the end of April, aggressive mounds of these little artichokes invade the fruit and vegetable stalls in the market. The remains of the prickly leaves are seen everywhere, outside houses in piles of sober green, sometimes overflowing into the middle of the streets. It takes many hours to pick clean a dish of these little artichokes; long practice is needed to avoid pricking oneself and it is impossible not to dirty one's hands. Take the precaution of soaking the hearts in water, otherwise they will turn black.

After all this, savouring the *tagine*, you will find it one of the most delicate and subtle of all.

For ten people.

Time required: three to four hours.

3 lb 6 oz shoulder and cutlets of mutton
9 lb wild artichokes
A ladle of olive oil
½ teaspoon ginger
A pinch of saffron pounded with salt
A pinch of pepper
1 chopped onion
Garlic to taste, about 2 cloves
A handful of salt

Put the oil, ginger, pepper, saffron, salt and onions in the *taoua*, stir with a wooden spoon adding little by little half a pint of water. Add the meat cut in large pieces and just cover it with water. Boil till the meat comes easily off the bone. Take out the meat. Then put in the artichokes; they should be cooked quickly, but must be watched carefully.

Arrange the meat covered with the artichoke hearts in the *tagine slaoui* with the sauce poured over the top. Put back on the fire for a minute. Serve very hot. This *tagine* may be garnished with olives and preserved lemons.

Other vegetables – broad beans, peas or cardoons –
can be used instead of artichoke hearts.

Summer Tagines

Tagine with Tomatoes

For ten people.

Time required: three hours.

Utensils: a *taoua* and a *tagine slaoui*.

4 ½ lb meat
4 ½ lb tomatoes
A ladle of olive oil
A pinch of cumin
A large pinch of ginger
Hot red soudania pepper to taste
½ teaspoon sweet red pepper
A pinch of ground black pepper
3 chopped cloves of garlic
2 chopped onions to be cooked with the meat,
1 lb 2 oz onions to be added with the tomatoes
A bunch of chopped parsley
A bunch of coriander
Salt to taste

Prepare the *tagine* in the usual way. Peel and seed the tomatoes and cut them into pieces. When the meat is half-cooked, put the parsley, the tomatoes and the onions in the *taoua*.

Various other vegetables — potatoes and peas, turnips, carrots and courgettes — can be used for this *tagine* instead of tomatoes. If you use carrots, add a few olives.

FRUIT TAGINES

Apples, pears, dates or raisins are the fruits used in these stews, the charm of which consists in the strange mixture of sweet fruits combined with the sharp shock of ginger.

A small locally grown pear is invariably used. The apples are of two kinds, one green and slightly acidic that ripens in the spring, the other, *lqim*, is red and yellow and sweet, with fruit no bigger than a plum, and comes from a wild apple tree which often produces two crops, the first at the beginning of the summer, and the second, less abundant, in the autumn.

Mutton or chicken can be used for these *tagines*, whichever you prefer.

TAGINE WITH QUINCES

For ten people.

Time required: three hours.

Utensils: a *taoua* and a *tagine slaoui*.

3 lb 6 oz mutton cut in pieces or 2 chickens
3 lb 6 oz quinces cut in half, seeded but not peeled

½ lb butter (or a mixture of butter and oil)
1 teaspoon ginger
1 teaspoon pepper
A pinch of salt
3 finely chopped onions
A bunch of chopped coriander

Put a chopped onion, the saffron, salt, ginger and the meat in the *taoua* and cover with water. When the meat is nearly cooked and the water three-quarters evaporated, add the two onions. Half an hour before serving put in the quinces, taking care they are not squashed; it is better to take out the meat before the fruit gets too soft and risks breaking.

Serve as usual in a *tagine slaoui*.

For *tagines* with quinces, apples or pears you can also put the fruit in a pan with a large piece of butter and simmer until the fruit is lightly caramelised.

Pears, apples, prunes and dates can be used instead of quinces. If you use prunes, don't soak them, just wash them.

Tagines With Fruit and Honey

Tagine with Prunes and Honey

For ten people.

Time required: three hours.

Utensils: a *taoua* and a *tagine slaoui*.

> 4 ½ lb mutton
> 2 lb 4 oz prunes
> A ladle of olive oil
> A pinch of ginger
> A pinch of saffron
> 1 onion
> A bunch of coriander
> Pepper to taste
> A pinch of salt
> A ladle of honey
> A whole cinnamon stick
> 2 spoonfuls orange flower water
> 1 oz sesame seeds browned in the oven
> without butter

Boil the meat, covered in water, in the *taoua* with

the ginger, saffron, salt, oil, coriander and cinnamon and onion. When the meat is well cooked and the liquor reduced to a thick sauce, take out the coriander and cinnamon stick, add the prunes, simmer for a quarter of an hour and then pour in the honey. Cook for another fifteen minutes on a slow fire. Add the orange flower water and bring to the boil.

Serve in a *tagine slaoui*, the prunes on top of the meat and with the sauce poured over the whole dish. Sprinkle with sesame.

Pears, quinces or apples can replace the prunes.

VEGETABLES

As a rule, Fassis do not care for vegetables. With the tip of a finger they will take and taste a little when it is well impregnated with meat juice from the *tagine*. The following recipes are used by people of modest fortune and the countryman who has come to work in the town. As you know how to prepare the meat with vegetables, you can cook different vegetables with the same recipes, leaving out the meat; saffron

– almost a necessity in the *tagine* – can be replaced by sweet red pepper which will give the sauce a rich warm colour; always use strong hot pepper and cumin to taste. Garlic, coriander, onion, fats, oil and butter (fresh or melted) are indispensable. The butter is often rancid, so less is needed. Oil which has turned sour rasps the throat, so a few drops are sufficient, which is a serious economy. Cook the vegetables in very little water so the sauce is always thick.

There is no rule for these *tagines*: each woman has her own way of cooking them, her *caïda* or custom, according to the place she comes from. Cooked carefully with good produce they are surprisingly appetising and make a pleasant change in the daily cooking.

BROAD BEANS

Fresh broad beans
Olive oil
Sweet red pepper
Hot red soudania pepper to taste
Cumin
Garlic
Salt
Coriander

Remove the shoots from the beans but do not peel them. Put enough water in the *taoua* to cover the beans, together with the oil, spices, garlic and coriander. When the water comes to the boil throw in the vegetables. Cook on a quick fire.

TOMATOES

Peel, seed and cut up the tomatoes. Cook with garlic, a little chopped onion, parsley, coriander, sweet and strong red pepper, oil but no water; a pinch of cumin may be added.

Aubergines and potatoes can be cooked in the same way.

MALLOW

In spring the women of Fez pick and sell bunches of leaves of a mallow that grows along the sides of the road. When cooked, these leaves are the colour of spinach, but, seasoned and garnished with olives and preserved lemons, they have a very hot and spicy flavour.

Time required: at least an hour and a half to allow the water to evaporate so that the dish can be kept for several days.

Utensils: a *tanjir*.

2 ½ lb cooked mallow leaves
A bunch of parsley
A few cloves of garlic
A good ladle of olive oil
1 teaspoon sweet red pepper
A little hot red soudania pepper pounded with salt
The juice of 3 lemons

The juice of 3 lemons
A bunch of chopped coriander
A small pinch of powdered cumin

Cut up the mallow leaves with the parsley and garlic. Steam in a pot with a perforated top as for *couscous*. Heat the olive oil in a *tanjir* and add the cooked mallow leaves, drained and pressed so that no water remains. Season with the pepper, lemon juice and coriander. Before taking off the fire mix in a little powdered cumin.

CAKES AND PASTRIES

Fassi pastries, which are generally complicated and difficult to make, are kneaded in the home and, like bread, baked outside the home in the oven or fried in oil. There are cakes in which the almond paste gives a note of luxury and refinement and honey its perfume, and simple fritters, light and golden, which are sold at the crack of dawn. There are rich pastries for feast days, beignets sticky with honey for the nights of Ramadan, the peasant's plain pancakes. Cakes make a gay display – along the streets pedlars offer sweetmeats of all colours. In some the sugar disguises the hashish, indulgence and philtre combined.

KAB EL GHZAL

For 50 large *kab el ghzal*.

Time required: three hours.

Utensils: a baking-sheet, a pestle and mortar, a pastry-board and a rolling-pin.

2 lb 4 oz almonds
10 oz sugar

1 lb 2 oz flour
5 oz butter
A few spoonfuls of orange flower water
½ oz pounded gum mastic
Water

Pound the almonds in the mortar with the sugar, add half the butter and perfume this paste with orange flower water. A mincing machine can be used nowadays, but the paste is smoother when pounded with the pestle.

Put the flour in the *gsaa*, make a hole in the

middle, melt the rest of the butter and pour it in with sufficient water to make a dough of the same consistency as bread dough. Knead energetically for at least twenty minutes.

Lightly grease the pastry board and rolling-pin and also your fingers. Take a piece of the dough, first roll it out, then stretch it with your hands until it is the thickness of a sheet of thin cardboard. Then make a sausage of the almond paste, roll the dough once round it and give it the form of a crescent. Lay it on the baking sheet and bake in a hot oven until lightly brown. If the dough swells too much, prick it with a pin.

GHORIBA

For 50 cakes.

Time required: two and a half hours.

Utensils: a *gsaa*, a fine sieve, a pestle and mortar and a baking sheet.

3 lb 6 oz sieved flour
1 lb 6 oz pounded and sifted sugar
1 lb 6 oz butter
½ oz gum mastic

Mix the flour, sugar and melted butter in the *gsaa* till the pastry is short and crumbly, kneading it well with the palm of your hand. With these quantities you can make about four dozen cakes about the size and shape of a macaroon. Bake in a hot oven.

GREEOUCH

Utensils: a *gsaa*, a *mqla*, a pastry board, a rolling-pin and a pastry cutter.

2 lb 4 oz flour
5 egg yolks
9 oz sugar
4 oz sesame seeds, of which 3 should be
finely pounded
Half a glass of vinegar
A bowl of bread yeast; this can be replaced by
baking powder or brewer's yeast
A pinch of salt
Groundnut oil
Honey

Knead in the *gsaa* the flour mixed with 3 oz of pounded sesame, the egg yolks, vinegar and sufficient oil to make the mixture a little firmer than the dough used for bread. Put on one side for several hours. Roll out the dough to a thickness of about ¼ inch.

Cut out pieces of about 8 by 5 inches with the pastry-cutter. Make six cuts in the paste to make seven strips leaving an edge of one inch top and bottom to hold it together. Lift the pastry with a finger through every other strip and with the other hand take one corner at the top and one corner at the bottom and press them together. Lay on the table in heaps of no particular shape. When all the cakes are ready, fry them in boiling oil till they are nicely browned.

Take out the *greeouch* with a skimmer, drain well and while they are still very hot plunge them into an earthenware bowl full of honey. Take out again

immediately and place on a dish. Sprinkle with sesame seeds. Golden, sticky and nourishing, they are one of the traditional cakes of Ramadan.

CHEBBAKIYA

This cake is made in large quantities every night during Ramadan.

To make it you will need fine flour, water, a little salt, yeast, a frying-pan full of oil, a pailful of honey, and ... a flower pot with a hole in the bottom, or a funnel.

Knead the flour, salt, water and yeast thoroughly, until you have a very soft dough. Put on one side for several hours. Now comes the sleight of hand which is amusing to watch. This is how I have seen it done in Fez Djedid, to the west of the old town.

Hold the flower pot filled with dough between your thumb and forefinger high above the pan of boiling oil, with your fourth finger blocking the hole. Remove your finger and trace quickly with the falling dough a flower with round petals about eight inches in diameter. Brown on both sides, turning it with an iron hook, then, while still boiling, dip it in the pailful of liquid honey for about one minute. The hollow parts of the well-risen dough will be filled with honey. When you crunch the scented and sugary *chebbakiya*, its thick essence will burst into your mouth.

BRIOUAT WITH RICE

The sheets of pastry are the same as for *bistilla*, with

one sheet for each cake. The stuffing is made of rice, put to soak in water and then cooked in sweetened milk with a small lump of butter. When the milk is completely absorbed the rice is cooked.

Fold the sheet of pastry in three with enough rice to form a little sausage roll in the shape of a cylinder, the edges stuck together with egg yolks. Fry in butter. Serve slightly warm, sprinkled with sugar and cinnamon.

M'hanncha

THE SNAKE

You have been offered this cake curled round like an adder on a silver-plated dish. Having tasted the pastry, frosty with sugar and shaded with cinnamon, you may find it heavy and insipid, but it melts in the mouth and is at the same time so crisp that you will go on tasting it till you can eat no more.

Fresh or reheated, believe me that this is food for the gods.

The pastry is the same as for *bistilla* (see pp. 59–60). The almond stuffing is similar to that for *kab el ghzal*, with a little cinnamon added.

Spread a sheet of pastry on the table, place the almond mixture about an inch thick down the centre, roll the sheet round the stuffing and curl it around itself in the form of a snail's shell. Brown in butter on both sides in a flat pan in the same way as *bistilla*.

Garnish with sugar and cinnamon. *M'hanncha* will keep several days. To crispen the pastry, reheat slightly before serving.

FEGGAS

Time required: half a day.

Utensils: a *gsaa* and a baking sheet.

4 ½ lb flour
9 oz sugar
1 oz yeast
1 ½ oz butter
1 dessertspoonful aniseed
2 tablespoonfuls orange flower water
Pounded gum mastic
A pinch of salt

*Tepid milk and water in a half and half mixture,
sufficient to obtain the consistency of
dough for bread*

Mix the flour, sugar, salt, yeast, aniseed, 1 oz of butter, milk and water in the *gsaa*. Knead well for about half an hour. Take a piece of dough about the size of a turkey's egg. Lightly grease the palms of your hands and roll the dough in the form of a small stick which you lay on the bread board. Use up all the dough in the same way and leave it to rise for at least two hours. Put in a hot oven and half cook. Take out of the oven. When they have cooled, cut the sticks into rounds about half an inch thick and put them back in the oven till well browned. The biscuits should be dry and crisp. When cool, put in a tin where they can be kept for months.

SFENJ

On a muddy and miserable winter's morning, the bench and brazier in the shop where fritters are made welcome and cheer me with their heat and strong-smelling squalor alleviated by the sweet scent of mint.

Abdallah brings in the tea. Sitting with the artisans in their *jellabas* on their way to Moulay Idriss and the workmen in jeans just off to their jobs, I savour this comforting breakfast taken by rich and poor alike with a glass of boiling mint tea into which they dip the hot *sfenj*.

Into the deep wide pan of boiling oil Abdallah

throws the rounds of dough, which, seized and turned over with an iron hook at the end of a wooden handle, become swollen, enlarged and browned on both sides; thrown on the scales then strung on a stick of *doum* they are handed to the little servant who takes this string of hot cakes home to his master for breakfast.

Abdallah has no time to explain, there are crowds waiting outside his shop, the *sfenj* are in danger of burning, but I know he was working till late at night so that the dough would rise and be ready at dawn.

I have marked down these proportions.

2 lb 4 oz flour
About a pint of warm water
A good pinch of salt
5 oz bread yeast from the day before or 1 oz beer yeast

Mix together the flour, salt, yeast and water. Knead well, add enough water to give the mixture a slightly more solid consistency than that used for making fritters. Put on one side for several hours. Heat the oil and when the dough has risen well take a piece and squeeze a quantity about the size of an egg through between the thumb and forefinger of your right hand, which must first be oiled; pierce the dough in the centre and turn it round rapidly with the fingers of the left hand and the thumb and forefinger of the right. Throw this disc into the boiling oil. It will swell and turn brown. Take care to turn it over with an iron hook when one side is cooked.

HALOUA RHIFA

This lavish cake served at marriages and circumcisions is a mountain of nougat topped with fresh butter. It is never made or sold in small quantities. At Chemmain, a continuation of the Great Taha, which leads to the heart of the *medina*, you will find it ready-made by specialists. Ask them to weigh several pounds, and after serving it at your reception you can return the remains and you will only pay for the difference in weight ... if this is not very hygienic, it is certainly convenient and economical!

Utensils: a *gsaa*, a pastry board and rolling-pin, a stick of smooth wood just over an inch in diameter, a frying-pan.

2 lb 4 oz flour
7 oz bread yeast
6 pints honey
A few spoonfuls of orange flower water
salt
3 oz butter
Water
Oil for frying

Knead the flour, yeast, salt and water in the same proportions as for bread, working it for a long time. Take a little of the dough and roll it out so that it is about a quarter of an inch thick. Then roll it round the smooth stick and slide it off into the pan of boiling oil. When all the dough is fried crush it in a dish with the rolling-pin. Heat the honey and mix it with the orange flower water and the crushed fried dough. Work the mixture well for half an hour. Roll out in a large flat dish so that it is about an inch thick. Leave on one side for twenty-four hours. Pile up in the shape of a cone in a deep dish, flattening the top with a lump of fresh butter.

With three fingers of the right hand take a small piece of cake and a little butter. Crunch it slowly. You will find it very similar to nougat.

JABAN

The maker of these sweetmeats walks around the streets carrying in front of him, like a church candle, his ribbon of sugar rolled round a bamboo cane or, stuck on a wooden tray, white macaroons decorated with an almond.

Caster sugar, egg-white and an ounce or two of gum mastic are all mixed together a long time before cooking. While eating these sweets stuffed with almonds or sesame seeds you will think of nougat, or meringues that have not quite come off.

The merchant of the Ben Safi souk who is renowned for these sweets is one of my friends. He has never consented to give me the recipe.

'You would teach the way of making *jaban* in the schools, and then how should I live, I, the master craftsman of these sweetmeats?'

I did not ask again, not wishing to lose his friendly greeting when passing by.

EL MAJOUN

Composing this mixture made of drugs and spices, hashish and honey, is an art. The proportions vary according to the science of the shopkeeper or the customer's requests. Certain grocers in the Attarine are renowned for their way of preparing a *majoun* and all the connoisseurs and those who are ill, impotent and old go to them.

Powdered acorns, honey, almonds browned in butter, specially prepared *ras el hanout*, cantharides, nuts, fresh butter, seeded raisins, ginger are all finely chopped and cooked on a slow fire until a thick jam-like consistency is formed. Stir in the quantity of hashish you consider necessary and make the mixture into little balls about the size of a pigeon's egg. Roll them in sesame seeds.

You will find *majoun* sold in the streets in the form of little balls ranging from dark to golden brown, sprinkled with sesame seeds and containing a strong proportion of hashish. These are bought by the poorer classes as a narcotic or aphrodisiac. In the shops where spices are sold you will find a *majoun* composed of finer and more expensive ingredients, but the best is home-made, cooked in wealthy households.

The cook in the home of one of my friends gave me her special recipe, which, she told me with a malicious smile, would keep me warm.

2 lb 4 oz almonds browned in butter
1 lb 2 oz walnuts
A handful of shelled acorns
2 lb 4 oz seeded raisins
Several cantharides
1 tablespoon ras el hanout
1 lb 2 oz honey
9 oz butter

Pound together the nuts, raisins and spices and then add the butter and honey. Cook as described earlier.

How much hashish did Dada Mbrika put in the *majoun*? I only saw her put a pinch, but I think she enlarged the dose when my back was turned.

FRUIT

Wipe the traces of *couscous* carefully from your fingers and help yourself to the season's fruit, brought in on a flat basket.

As soon as the winter is over you will find medlars with their enormous dark amber-coloured stones, thick skin and acid pulp.

In May you will savour the *mechmech*, the little apricot which is better and sweeter than the large ones from Spain.

Then, at the beginning of summer come small wild cherries from Sefrou which are dark and sweet, fresh, hard pears and purple and yellow plums.

These fruits, delivered to the shops in long narrow baskets of plaited reeds, covered only with leaves or bunches of herbs, come from trees which have not been grafted and, except for the cherries, are grown in the gardens of Fez or in orchards around the ramparts.

We must not forget the mulberry trees which border many of the avenues leading out of the town. Women and children hit the trees with bamboo canes – greatly to the detriment of young shoots – knocking down the fruit which they gather up in bundles of gay, multi-coloured cretonne.

On the pavement, the mulberries, a mass of purple and white, are laid on a bed of greenery. They are offered to the children and the *msaken* or beggars for a few francs, as the *lqim* will be offered later on, tiny apples the colour of crab apples, but soft and sweet in contrast with the larger apples which are green and insipid, just good enough to put in a spicy *tagine*.

And here are the first figs swollen with seeds, forerunners of those of midsummer displayed in such quantities on the fruit stalls with the marvellous golden white grapes of Lemta that will remind you of the finest French chasselas. They are so much better than the later grapes, pale purple turning to green, as big as the small wild plums, which are more decorative than edible. The peaches are green, hard, always maggoty and quite worthless.

MELONS AND WATER-MELONS

On a stifling summer evening during the *chergui*, the dry and burning east wind, strolling in the shadow of the walls of the Lycée Moulay Idriss and choosing a melon or water-melon for dessert is one of the refreshing pleasures of all the social classes of the town.

The air is saturated with dust, the constant ringing of the water carrier's bell is exasperating. Acetylene lamps light up each pile of fruit. One or two water-melons are cut, a gash like an open wound proving the quality of the fruit. Choosing a water-melon is an art. You must weigh it, sound it to judge the degree of ripeness, smell it to make sure of its perfume. Naturally you do all this with at least ten, and then finally return to your first choice.

A smaller heap of rough-skinned melons, the colour of ripe corn, excudes an odour so strong as to be almost sickening. These are the melons grown by the Maïa tribe at the foot of the Zerhoun Mountains. They are treated in the same way as the others, smelt, weighed and tapped.

At last, slowly, arms filled with his double choice, the Fassi goes home. Yasmina will plunge a large knife into the water-melon to divide it and empty out the black seeds. When cut up everybody will take a piece, biting into the fresh red pulp which fills the mouth with its sweet juice, the drops running down their fingers.

The melon will be offered and eaten in the same way. Though not quite like a cantaloupe, the melons grown by the Maïa have a strong sweet flavour.

At night Yasmina will empty into the already bursting dustbin outside the door the seeds and pulpy rind that will attract the flies which infest the air.

OTHER FRUIT.

The only bananas are large, floury and without any taste.

Prickly pears on a barrow are displayed to the

passer-by, opened with a quick turn of the knife and eaten then and there.

On the stalls you will also see a rather sordid display of jujubes, seeds of marrow and melon, sweet acorns from the forest of Mamora and grilled chick-peas. All these are nibbled throughout the day by children and idle women.

In the autumn small baskets are garnished with round bright red fruit no bigger than strawberries, on a string of *doum*. Children love these arbutus berries, probably more for their colour than for their insipid flavour.

The ruby-coloured seeds of pomegranates are taken out and served on a dish with a sweet juice perfumed with orange flower water.

In the winter a plate of thin-skinned oranges from the valleys of the Rif or the thicker-skinned ones from Ghafsai will give you as much if not more pleasure than the finest fruit from California.

Nuts from the Rif or the Atlas Mountains, almonds served grilled and salted, dried figs and raisins from the Senhaja tribe served with dates from the Tafilalet – the early ones light and small – are like those from the Algerian oases, but the later ones, large, dark and pulpy, better for keeping.

If you have the courage, try some of the dates piled together and compressed into a sort of nougat. The seller will cut through the mass of pulp and stones with the stroke of a sharp bayonet. These dates give one the feeling of crunching the very sands of the oasis.

Fruit eaten in the streets of Fez, or savoured at the

end of a meal is not of an especially fine variety, but, thanks to the sun which has ripened it, it has much value for its sweetness and the quality of its scent.

DRINKS

WATER

In this town the 'gift of God' is water. Water flows everywhere in dirty rivers, imprisoned in drains which are always being repaired, under the houses and over the chain pumps. Each palace has its fountain and pond, nearly every dwelling has a well with running water, some renowned for their cool purity.

Branches of the River Fez that turn the mills are also used as drains. There is a monotonous wailing of the water wheels, the sound of waterfalls mixing with the noises of the street.

Fassis like spring water put to cool in a water-bottle with a glass that serves as a stopper. Each passer-by can quench his thirst while evoking the name of Allah.

Before the coming of modern water installations, the water carrier with his goatskin or barrels on his donkey's back brought the water and poured it into large jars placed at the kitchen door by those who were without drinking water.

Nowadays for those who have not been able to install in their houses the water brought from Ain Chkeff, a spring a few miles from Fez, the public fountains, invaded by crying, pushing children, splashing themselves as they fill their buckets, are more important than the picturesque water-carrier in his well-known costume. He seems more use as a model for tourists, as he offers in his brass bowl that precious liquid with a rose petal or an orange blossom floating on top.

MILK OF ALMONDS

On feast days this is the drink of the rich people of Fez. The proportions vary, but these seem good to me.

1 lb 2 oz almonds
2 pints water

7 oz sugar
Orange flower water to taste

Pound the almonds into a smooth paste. Dilute the sugar with the water and blend with the almond paste. Pass through a fine sieve. Serve iced.

THE ART OF MAKING
AND DRINKING TEA

We have come to the end of the meal. Over the
couscous the conversation languishes. Fruit has
refreshed throats burning with strong spices. The
table is taken away, the mattresses put back in their
places along the walls. The serving girl has passed
the basin and ewer, pouring the warm purifying

water over our greasy fingers. Mouths rinsed, hands washed, the guests get up slowly, only to sink back once more on the divans and lean against the gold-embroidered cushions surrounded with silks, muslins and velvets, eyes lost in restful contemplation of the painted ceiling.

There is an atmosphere of calm satisfaction, not excited by wines and spirits.

It is pleasant to be in this long, colourful room with its mosaics and painted beams. We appreciate it all lazily through half-closed eyelids. In the marble patio the *zellijes* of the fountains shimmer with water and sun. The only sound is of falling water. Near the fountain a bouquet of flowers arranged in a fantastic geometrical design forming a cone on a round tray of plaited reeds gives a note of refined elegance. In their bamboo cages doves coo and goldfinches answer them, piercing the lightness of the air. The round-bellied cat sleeps in the sun. Like a streak of lightning a lively child runs barefoot across the patio. For one second he throws a curious glance towards the master's guests; he is quickly seized and carried off by the *dada*.

Our host has placed the sweet-smelling wood in the incense burner. Each guest bends over the heavenly smoke with the hood of his burnous pulled down over his face, impregnating his garments with the precious scent. Rose water is passed round in embossed silver bottles to refresh face, neck, and hands.

Yasmina, skirts tucked up above her voluminous trousers, a rose behind her ear, brings in the pastries veiled in muslin, then the carved boxes containing tea and sugar, and the bowl of mint. She offers the silver-plated tray with its coloured glasses to each guest. Then like a smoking engine the samovar appears, steam emerging from its spout. The almost religious ceremony can now begin. Everyone gazes in silence.

I have tried to seize the secret possessed by each child born in Fez ... the art of making tea.

TEA

It is interesting to know how the Moroccan, who in bygone days drank only infusions of wormwood and mint, came to mix them with tea.

If, since the beginning of the nineteenth century, rich Fassis occasionally drank this beverage, it is only since 1854 at the time of the Crimean War, when the blockade of the Baltic drove British merchants to seek new markets for their wares and led them to dispose of important stocks of tea in Tangier and Mogador, that this drink became common. Since then its popularity has never ceased to grow and it is now the daily and universal drink throughout Morocco.

There are many varieties of tea and the price varies according to the quality. The leaves, coarse or fine, scented or insipid, sometimes containing opium, can be infused alone or with the addition of sprigs of mint.

MINT

The only mint that can be used is *mentha viridis*. The best quality, dark and with firm stalks, comes from Meknès or the Zerhoun. Mint grown in the gardens of Fez is less scented.

Fassis of all classes on their way home in the evening will stop and buy a few sprigs from the seller of mint squatting behind the mass of dark green in which he has stuck a red rose here and there.

Wormwood or sage can be infused with the tea in the winter when it is hard to find mint. These aromatic plants are helpful for soothing a stomach ache. Verbena, sweet marjoram, sweet basil and amber are used in the same way, but less often, as is peppermint, known as *roumia*. In season orange blossom accompanies the mint. An infusion with balls of amber is rare and refined. The sugar used is a loaf of cane sugar. Honey and brown sugar are things of the past. The teapot is of the finest silver plate. Two are needed for receptions. Teapots of rustic pottery or flowered china are rarely used nowadays.

Tea-making is a gift of God, a gift that cannot be acquired. There are no proportions, no rules for making tea, no two glasses ever taste the same. The quality of the leaves is of an infinite variety – before the war I was told of more than sixty sorts. The quantity and quality of the mint, everything counts in this infusion. I will try to teach you to make this green tea in a way that I hope will be drinkable without presuming to reach the ultimate perfection where the scented mint brings to the bitterness of the tea its fresh and piquant flavour.

The real connoisseurs who possess the most renowned kinds of tea, never put mint in the first teapot. The *caïda* or custom of three consecutive pots is dying out as tea and sugar are too expensive.

The proportions that follow are for ten persons. For a teapot containing 1½ pints heat the pot, pour in ½ glass of boiling water, rinse, turning the teapot round quickly, and throw away this water, which serves to wash away the dust and a little of the bitterness. Put in 1½ tablespoons of tea. A handful of mint leaves and stalks and 5 or 6 oz of sugar are needed. Fill up the teapot with boiling water from the samovar. Leave to draw for seven to eight minutes, stir with a spoon, put a little in a glass and taste, adding sugar if necessary. Take care that the mint does not rise above the water as this will spoil the taste of the tea.

For a reception two teapots are prepared with the same infusion. Hold one in each hand high above the glass and pour in the liquid from both pots at the same time. Here again a certain sleight of hand is required, but it is worth practising for the dramatic effect produced.

The second teapotful. While your guests are enjoying the first infusion, the second will be prepared. Leave the mint and tea in the pot and add another teaspoon of tea, a few leaves of mint and about 5 oz of sugar. Add boiling water. Leave to draw and keep hot till the mint rises to the surface.

Stir. Taste to see if more sugar is needed.

Yasmina will fill each glass with this tea, which is thick with mint and darker in colour.

For the third teapotful, the same process is followed, but mint may be replaced by wormwood.

While drinking, tongues are loosened at last. The time has come for small talk and gossip.

I have described the hour after the meal in a rich man's house when everything turns round the sacred rite of tea-making. But you must not forget that for the entire population this very sweet drink forms the basis of its food, the source of much of its energy. Tea is drunk at the slightest pretext every hour of the day, consumption curbed only by the cost.

During the day the workman is satisfied to eat just bread and olives, but he will boil water between two stones and produce from a rag everything necessary for this drink: a little tea, large splinters of sugar loaf, leaves of wormwood or mint. And there, sitting cross-legged on the ground, he will sip the tea with a pleasure which for a few minutes makes him equal to the wealthy merchant. At home, in the evening, after a simple meal comes the hour of calm and relaxation; the reunited family sips the boiling tea noisily while discussing the day's doings, politics and their own hopes and aspirations. Then with perfumed breath they will fall asleep on the mats where they have been sitting, dreaming of a paradise where all the rivers flow with precious scented tea.

The peasant also drinks tea. The countryman's repast is very frugal, biscuits made of oats or maize, *lben*, butter, fruit and always weak tea thickened with mint and sweetened with sugar.

When the Berber in his tent produces out of his painted tins the dearly bought tea, he will serve it to you strong and very sweet, along with heavy cakes and rancid butter.

AROMATICS

Fassis have a very acute sense of smell and are partial to scents. After a good meal, the exhalation of aromatics mingled with the sprinkling of rose water ... sensuality ... refinements of luxury ... but also the wish to drive away the *djinn* and as protection against the evil eye, and to attract good spirits.

Lift up the openwork lid of the brass incense burner and throw in according to your choice *jaoui el mekkaoui*, benzoin from Mecca, the resin of a tree, perfume composed of amber and musk, *jaoui soudani*, benzoin from the Sudan of a very inferior quality, or sandalwood.

THE DISTILLATION OF ORANGE BLOSSOM AND ROSE PETALS

Orange flower water and rose water are best home-made. That bought in the shops is certainly not as strong.

It is in the dark kitchen that you must watch the working of the still, the brazier, the mass of red copper, the brightly dressed servant, the whiteness of orange blossom and the softness of rose petals which produce the intoxicating smell. The whole atmosphere is violent and mysterious, which is doubtless necessary for the distillation of these subtle perfumes.

A *kanoun* and a *qettara* are the essential equipment. The *qettara* or copper still is divided into three: the lower part an ordinary *taoua* in which the water is boiled; on top the *kskas* with holes in it, to hold the flowers, and finally the *qettara*, a receptacle with two tubes, one to take the steam from the water which has just come through the petals and let it cool, the other used for emptying the still when the water intended for the purpose of condensing into steam is reheated. In a bottle placed at the end of the first tube you will see the perfumed water falling drop by drop.

With 6 lb 12 oz of blossom or petals you will obtain 12 pints of this precious liquid, ready for use in the kitchen or as toilet water.

NEZAHA

Picnic? Literary and musical assembly? Rural pleasure trip?

May and June bring fine days at the beginning of the summer. The grass has not yet run to seed, the beans smell of honey, the pears are already big, the plums well formed, the leaves of the pomegranate tree are red and glowing. The running *seguia* reflects the patches of sunlight through the branches. These are the gardens of Fez enclosed by reeds and periwinkles.

The porters have already put the carpets, mattresses and cushions in gay masses of colour on the ground.

It is on these joyous mornings that Fassis like to meet, happy to leave their usual occupations and their families behind for a day. The violinist and the mandolin player bring their instruments, the dilettante nonchalantly carries a cage with a canary.

Stretched out and relaxed in complete and happy abandon in front of the samovar, this party will exchange ideas all day; the poet will read his verses, an Andalusian *motet* will be played on the violin, the mandolin will reply, the singer will improvise a song.

And when the hot sun at its zenith has calmed all this joy and gaiety for a while, the *zarzaia* or porters will appear in a long procession, carrying on their heads the huge dishes with their pointed lids which keep the food hot. With sharpened appetites they will judge critically the *tagines* prepared with the utmost care by the mistress of the house and her servants, who know that the quality of the food will be appreciated and the slightest failing noticed and criticised.

I have never been able to make my friends tell me what means most to them during this day: the feasting or the joys of the spirit. As in all things, the whole must be perfect to procure the greatest pleasure.

Restaurants

The inhabitants of Fez are very hospitable and will entertain strangers, friends or relations equally well. There is no place where the saying, '*Les amis de nos amis sont nos amis*' is more true.

It is therefore unnecessary for the visiting manufacturer or tradesman to book rooms; he will always find an open door somewhere, a mat to lie on, a *tagine* in which to dip his bread, above all tea to sip and inhale while listening to the news and gossip. There are also many men, born in Fez and now scattered all over Morocco as businessmen, lawyers and professors; these children of Fez are welcomed with joy when they return home.

But there are restaurants in the *medina*, where the rich *fellah* who has come to buy spices and cloth, will find *tagines* simmering in copper stew pans and snowy heaps of *couscous* in huge dishes, a display of chickens golden with saffron, fried shad, delicious pancakes and all kinds of pastries with honey and almonds. From the street he can see all the food in bright copper pots cooking on the large kitchen stove decorated with *zellijes*.

Simpler food shops are to be found towards Bab

Sensla, where you will find dishes of mallow and fennel garnished with olives and lemons, where hard-boiled eggs sprinkled with cumin surround the greasy pan of oil in which small fish are frying. The seller of iced *lben* and fruit juice in glazed earthenware jars. Great pans like vats where the traditional *harira* simmers all day long and is served, when the day's work is over, to the labourer come alone to town. All this simple rustic food is offered in displays protruding onto the road, protected from the swarms of flies by the horse-tail mounted on a stick that is waved to and fro mechanically by a sleepy child.

The seller of *brochettes* is seated like a buddha in front of the brazier. Seductive smoky exhalations from the meat will sharpen your appetite and you will buy half a *ksra* in which to hide the grilled *brochette*.

Bare-chested, the maker of fritters, in his empty shop, kneads the dough which must rise at dawn. Near the Qaraouine in the city-centre the pastry cooks will offer you, on painted patterned plates, their multi-coloured cakes, coated with honey or sprinkled with sugar.

You may taste these soups, brochettes, *tagines* and pastries. If the oil and butter are of a good quality you will be pleasantly surprised. Although not to be compared with the same food cooked in the home, the unexpectedness of these snacks and the atmosphere of the place will please you as much as the dishes themselves.

CAFÉS

In the Najjarine neighbourhood where the carpenters work, built up against a vine is the little café where the old craftsmen can only enter bent double. Like in a doll's house, the low door touches the ceiling and there is only just room for Moulay Ahmed to sit down.

Hunched up on a low stool, he goes automatically through the gestures of tea-making – tea, mint, sugar, looking after the brazier and always keeping the water on the boil. For each customer Moulay Ahmed prepares the infusion in a small long-handled teapot of blackened metal, pours it into the glasses carried in a wire basket that the *zarzai* or porter will distribute quickly among the shop-keepers and artisans of the district, scenting the air as he passes with the sprigs of mint that crown each glass.

I owe these memories, Moulay Ahmed, to you. I wonder did you ever suspect the joy it gave me to sit outside your door on the cedar bench, leaning over to watch you work and to listen to you ...? Above

all to listen. You taught me more than all my professors – your language, the accent of your town, the everyday life of its people.

And when, one day, in your place I found only your son, I knew I had lost a friend.

Cafés for the idle, dreamers and students. All along the banks of the river in the gardens of Boujloud, amid the languid wailing of the chain pumps, the swaying of the weeping willows and in the bluish light coming through the wooden latticework, you can drink weak tea, strongly flavoured with mint.

Cafés towards Seffarine whose walls are decorated with naïve drawings and where draughts and cards are played while strong tea is enjoyed.

Cafés in the district of Moulay-Abdallah where the atmosphere is sultry. Here the smokers of *kif* are to be found lying stretched out on mats.

Qahaouajia, the cafés of Fez, where nothing is served but tea, fruit juices or Coca Cola ... each one reflects the soul of its neighbourhood.

All are worth visiting, their diversity will amuse you. Through them you will get to know, better than from learned books, the multifarious inhabitants of this city.

THE MARKETS AND FOOD SHOPS OF FEZ

The wholesale market of Bab-Jiaf, like every auction, is crowded with vegetables and fruit. The surrounding streets are obstructed with vans and carts, porters, buyers and sellers discussing with loud cries understood by no one but themselves. Donkeys laden with *doum* baskets trotting as quickly as they can, carrying food for the inhabitants down into the heart of the *medina*.

The tranquillity of the *fondouks* or hotels stuffed with provisions: tea, sugar, flour, cereals, biscuits. Habits of an over-populated town, survivals of a time when roads were not always safe for transport.

In different districts, stalls displaying piles of vegetables and fruit.

Grocer's shops where the sugar loaves wrapped in blue paper line the walls at the back of the shop.

Cake shops with pastries of astonishing colours.

Flour and semolina merchants in their white woollen shirts and bonnets.

The street of the butchers with their display of shapeless portions of meat. Sheep hung up with

pieces hacked off without any technique, as though some wild animal had torn at them. Pale fats, huge chunks of purple camel's meat.

The block where the seller of *kefta* endlessly and tirelessly chops the mottled meat together with the aromatic spices.

The sombre cavern of the coal merchant, where coal is weighed on scales with a long arm, by a man from the Sahara. Coal which is always called *el biad* (the white) by Moroccans.

Attarine, the street which makes the Berber's eye gleam with envy. A street of intoxicating scents and colours. Spices without which the *tagine* would only be a stew, the *mechoui* an ordinary roast joint.

Shad from the Sebou in pairs, their tails trailing in the dust.

Bewildered chickens with open beaks cluster round the seller seated in the gutter.

Some streets are encumbered with pedlars selling inferior wares from carts or sometimes just laid on the ground.

Women returning from their work of weeding in the fields offer the passer-by four onions, ten over-ripe tomatoes, a few sprigs of mint, five lemons. Stolen goods or a gift?

Bunches of mallow leaves, fennel flowers, thistles stripped of their leaves, picked from land lying fallow and brought in sacks by the peasant to be emptied on the pavement; bundles of cardoon; piles of oranges.

In the spring, under Bab Smarin, bowls of fermented milk with lumps of butter floating on top, basins of steamed *couscous* ready to be moistened with *lben*.

Some years there are grilled locusts that look like prawns.

The sellers of green and acid olive oil.

Ksra piled one on top of the other and kept warm beneath a woollen cloth, one placed on top and cut in half to show the quality of the flour.

Nougat carried around on a bamboo cane.

Small trades, miniscule profits and shoddy merchandise for poor people.

Street cries: 'American sweets ... grilled peanuts ... *jaban* ... *jaban*.'

And always the smells ... spices, oil, grilled meats smoking in the open air.

Narrow streets lined with shops. Smells ... cries ... hustling and hurrying ... dust ... heat ... vertigo.

To do a day's marketing is to be initiated into the life of Fez.

MECHOUI

This famous way of cooking mutton does not actually come into the recipes used by the Fassi, so I am giving it as an extra apart from Fez and its cooking.

Choose a young sheep – fat, but not too big.

'*Bsmillah*' – plunge the knife into the carotid artery and let the blood spurt out to the last drop. Wash the gash in the throat seven times. Make a hole with the point of the knife just above the knee joint of one of the back legs between flesh and skin. Put a stick in this hole and, turning it round, start to loosen the skin. Blow through this opening until the air gets to the fore legs and makes them stick up. The sheep will then swell and stiffen as though it had been a long time in water.

Quickly, while an assistant stops up the hole, cut the skin between the legs and skin the sheep as you would a rabbit. Be careful not to cut the trotters or the head, and respect the horns.

Hang up the hide to clean it, put aside the liver and the heart, then hang them up. Give the tripe to the women, who will scrape, rinse and put it to dry. Singe and clean the head and trotters.

Take a pick-axe and a spade. Dig a hole about four feet long and eighteen inches wide and sixteen inches deep. Place two forked sticks at each end. Light a good fire in this hole and let it burn.

When the fire is covered with light ashes impale the sheep right through from tail to throat on a strong stick long enough to rest on the two forks, which serve as an axis.

Cook slowly, throwing a little earth on the fire when it becomes too hot or, if it is not hot enough, add charcoal from a brazier placed near by.

Have to hand 2 lb 4 oz of butter and a little salt and pepper. A rag tied round a branch is used as a brush and every ten minutes the mutton is brushed over while being turned on this improvised spit.

During this time cook the liver lightly and prepare

the *boulfaf* as indicated in the chapter on *brochettes*. Grill just before serving.

Five hours are necessary for the skin to become like a carapace, crackly and dark, while the flesh remains juicy and unctuous. The choicest morsels to pick out, at the risk of burning your fingers, are the kidneys and the meat on the shoulders.

Place the animal on a large deep copper tray, arranging it with care, the four legs tucked underneath, the head raised, if necessary with the aid of a piece of bamboo, the horns well up. Stick the *brochettes* of *boulfaf* like arrows down the sheep's back.

Serve with saucers of salt, powdered cumin and red pepper.

THE CORPORATION OF COOKS

This book would be incomplete without mentioning the corporation of cooks, an organisation with an *amine* or chief at its head, and under him the members, both men and women.

For marriages, circumcisions and receptions the ordinary cook kept by a well-off family will not be able to prepare the numerous dishes for feasts to which several hundred guests are invited. So the head of the corporation is called upon to hire out the necessary cooks and to place them under the direction of a man who the *amine* and the host hold responsible for the quality of the repast.

It is impossible to find women more superstitious, inquisitive or gossipy than these cooks. They know all the weaknesses of their masters, every scandal in the big houses where they serve and they are sure to spread their tittle-tattle from kitchen to kitchen.

Gathered round the brazier and copper pans they make the children tremble with their stories of devils and witches. At the end of the feast, when the guests, satiated with the rich food and strong spices, sink back on the divans with a sigh, the cook squatting in the kitchen, her black face shining under the fringed scarf tied round her head, the whites of her eyes and teeth gleaming as she sucks the last bones of the very last chicken, will tell the frightened yet delighted children tales of the misdeeds of *Aïcha qandicha*, who, as everyone knows, has goat's feet and one eye in the middle of her forehead.

Each cook has her speciality, the *tagine* in which she will put the perfect quantity of spices, from recipes handed down through generations by word of mouth. They all know that it is better never to undertake the preparation of any dish without first having driven away the *djinn* who will spoil the sauces and burn the meat ... a few grains of benzoin scattered over the brazier and these disasters, which make the *amine* bad tempered, can be avoided. Paid very little, they are fed and they may take away the offal from the poultry, which they can sell. The number of these extras will be about thirty, the women specialists in making the *bistilla* only eight. A long apprenticeship is needed to acquire the supple wrist for throwing the dough in the correct way. They bring with them the utensils necessary for making this complicated pastry dish.

There are five chefs, expert cooks, who are there more to direct and command the hired women than for the actual cooking. It is they who plan the menu with the master of the house and decide on the quantities of food needed for making the various dishes.

The *amine*, the accomplished head of the

corporation, knows all the traditions of the culinary arts of Fez. He is constantly consulted, it is he who provides and sends the staff of servants for each reception. He is paid a deposit and hires out the china dishes for the *bistilla* and the copper pans and *taoua*.

The shopkeepers of Moulay Idriss retain the right to hire out the glasses, boxes, teapots and embossed brass and silver trays.

PUBLISHER'S NOTE

Madame Guinaudeau's book was not written in the age of the microwave nor in a culture in which the number of people at a table rarely exceeds four. Although most of the recipes in this book are easily made, there is in Madame Guinaudeau's writing much reference to lengthy preparation and slow cooking. While food-processors and other conveniences will allow time to be saved in preparing these dishes, we have left the recipes as they were originally written in the Morocco of the 1950s, confident that readers can adapt them for their own use in a modern kitchen.

Recipes in the original edition of this book are for eight or ten, occasionally even fifteen or twenty guests, and we have not sought to change them to the four or six people deemed to be the statistical dining average in most modern cookbooks. Some of the recipes in *Traditional Moroccan Cooking* are elaborate and only worth preparing for as many guests as can be squeezed around the table.

Although there is not a substantial Moroccan community in either Britain or the United States, it should not be difficult to find the ingredients needed in Moroccan cooking. Greek, Turkish, Indian, Pakistani and Middle Eastern shops sell almost all the herbs, spices and other ingredients called for here. Readers with access to such shops – almost anyone in a large town or city in Britain or North America – should not encounter untoward problems in finding the ingredients called for by Madame Guinaudeau. *Couscous* may now be bought, pre-cooked, in packets, as can the filo pastry used in a *bistilla* and other recipes in this book, and readers should take advantage of these and other time-saving innovations. Orange flower water, used here in both cake and *tagine* recipes, is often used in cake icing and may be bought quite easily; it may also be found in Middle Eastern shops.

Utensils, however, are more problematic. It is almost impossible to buy a *tagine slaoui*, called for in many of these recipes, in either Britain or the United States, but fire-proof Spanish or Portuguese earthenware casseroles will make an acceptable substitute; if they cannot be found, a heavy enamel casserole will have to suffice. It is very difficult to make a traditional *couscous* satisfactorily without a *couscousière*, and these can be bought in well-stocked specialist kitchenware shops in Britain and North America. A large roasting tin makes a reasonable substitute for a *gsaa*, and readers should have litle difficulty in adapting other easily obtained kitchen equipment for Madame Guinaudeau's recipes. Those fortunate enough to visit Morocco, or parts of France with a North African population, should take the opportunity to buy some of the equipment called for in this book as well as stocking up their larders.

We are most grateful to Vicky Hayward, Angus Mitchell, M'hammed Phaytan, Claudia Roden and Sally Singer for their advice and assistance with this new edition.

INDEX

CASABLANCA CUISINE
French North African Cooking

Aline Benayoun

Casablanca Cuisine recreates the lost world of the *pieds noirs*, French settlers in North Africa, and is a perfect example of food as the meeting point of cultures. Offering such delights as chicken with olives, tuna with red peppers and capers, and date and almond nougat, this is the first ever book on this healthy and sophisticated cuisine.

Borrowing ideas and ingredients from their Arab neighbours, the *pieds noirs* learned to cook meat with fruit and created delicacies such as lamb with pears, chicken with quinces, and meatballs with lemon. Combining European vegetables with a North African spice, they made a beetroot and carrot salad with cumin, while in concocting a mint soup they took the most typical of local herbs and made a refreshing soup of the classic French style.

Like all North African cuisines, *pied noir* cooking places great importance on fresh ingredients, and Aline Benayoun presents a full range of tasty and nutritious vegetable, fish and meat dishes as well as salads and *pied noir* versions of couscous.

'Written from the heart, a delightful book about family cooking with all the tantalising flavours of Morocco. It is also a precious record of the vanished world of the *pied noir* communities of North Africa.'
Claudia Roden

paperback

ROMAN COOKERY
Ancient Recipes for Modern Kitchens

Mark Grant

Roman Cookery unveils one of Europe's last great culinary secrets – the food eaten by the ordinary people of ancient Rome. Based on olive oil, fish, herbs and vegetables, it was the origin of modern European cooking and, in particular, what we now call the Mediterranean diet. Mark Grant, classics teacher and researcher *extraordinaire*, has unearthed recipes like tuna wrapped in vine leaves, olive oil bread flavoured with cheese, and quinces in wine. He presents unknown delights such as honey and sesame pizza, eggs poached in wine, and ham in red wine and fennel sauce.

Meat was just an occasional treat for most Romans, who were however great lovers of herbs, and *Roman Cookery* offers a range of herb sauces and purées, originally made with a pestle and mortar, but here adapted, like all these dishes, to be made with modern kitchen equipment. Grant also provides the reader with a fascinating explanation of the cultural values ascribed to Roman food and of the social context in which it was eaten and enjoyed.

'A fascinating book for all who love Italian cooking and an invaluable addition to the Italophile cook's library. The inspirational ancient recipes, with their intriguing and unusual combinations of fresh herbs and vegetables with bread and hard cheeses, naturally complement the modern Italian food we love.'
Rose Gray

paperback

CLASSIC JAMAICAN COOKING
Traditional Recipes and Herbal Remedies

Caroline Sullivan

Okra, plantains, sweet potatoes and mangoes: these and the other essential ingredients of Jamaican cooking are now widely available in Britain and North America, bringing the island's delicious cooking within anyone's reach.

Covering all aspects of Jamaican cuisine from soups to preserves, fish to ices, *Classic Jamaican Cooking* also presents a range of traditional herbal remedies and drinks. With recipes as varied as plantain tart and okra soup, salt fish patties and coconut ice-cream, this book dispels forever the myth that Jamaican cooking begins with curried goat and ends with rice and peas.

Needing only occasional modification for the modern reader ('Take seven gallons of rum, three gallons of seville orange juice . . .'), Caroline Sullivan brings alive the wealth and variety of the island's food. With its blending of African and European influences, Jamaican cooking rests on a foundation of tropical fruits and vegetables, and the author draws out the full range of their flavours in one of the New World's tastiest cuisines.

'A wealth of very good recipes'
Frances Bissell, *The Times*

'Wonderful ideas that will appeal to adventurous cooks'
Lindsey Bareham

'A useful addition to your kitchen library'
The Voice

paperback

BENGALI COOKING
Seasons and Festivals

Chitrita Banerji

We are just beginning to appreciate the culinary diversity of the Indian subcontinent's numerous regions. Bengal is home to both Hindus and Muslims and her people farm the fertile Ganges delta for rice and vegetables and fish the region's myriad rivers. As recipes for fish in yoghurt sauce, chicken with poppy seeds, aubergine with tamarind, duck with coconut milk and other delights in *Bengali Cooking: Seasons and Festivals* all testify, Bengal has one of Asia's most delicious and distinctive cuisines.

This highly original book takes the reader into kitchens in both Bangladesh and the Indian state of West Bengal by way of the seasons and religious and other festivals that have shaped the region's cooking. Chitrita Banerji offers her readers the wonderful recipes of Bengali home-cooking – dals, fish, vegetables and kedgerees – rather than the standard fare of Indian restaurants. Hers is much more than a cookbook: it is also a vivid and deeply felt introduction to the life, landscape and culture of the Bengali people.

'Delightful ... written with a rare grace and zest'
Matthew Fort, *The Guardian*

'Chitrita Banerji gives her readers a keen appetite for the subtle flavours of India's most interesting region'
Paul Levy

paperback

COOKING IN TEN MINUTES

Edouard de Pomiane

300 uncomplicated *and* delicious recipes by France's most creative cookery writer, the witty, irreverent and super-efficient Edouard de Pomiane. Whizzing from stove to table, and still keeping everything under control, he delights us with his joy in cooking and with his belief that good food need not be the sole preserve of people with vast amounts of time and money to spend. This book is a must for anyone who leads a busy life but is determined to create the space in which to eat well.

'A good teacher, philosopher and a very happy cook. He will pour light on both your cooking and attitude to life.'
Raymond Blanc

'Both timeless and timely, Pomiane's stylish good sense never dates.'
Geraldene Holt

'Not only a great chef, he was also a philosopher with an hilarious sense of fun ... You will love him and his writing.'
Jennifer Patterson

'An inspirational energy and joy in cooking.'
The Guardian

paperback

FINE ENGLISH COOKERY

Michael Smith

English cooking is currently enjoying a renewed vitality after decades spent in the shadow of European and other cuisines. Michael Smith's highly acclaimed book is centred on eighteenth-century recipes, but also delves back into Tudor and Stuart kitchens, and his skill in adapting old dishes for the contemporary cook puts almond soup, caveached sole, and asparagus and bacon fraze within easy reach of today's reader.

Traditionally, English cooking was generous in its use of herbs and spices and adventurous in its combining of flavours, and Michael Smith's wide-ranging research uncovers dishes with a surprisingly modern air: mustard soup, salmon in red wine, and gooseberry and rosemary ice-cream, for example, sit alongside classic potted meats and fish.

For too long, breakfast and tea have been seen as the only meals at which English cooking has anything to offer the world. This refreshingly contemporary collection of classic recipes proves once and for all that the inventiveness and diversity of English food deserve to be recognised - and enjoyed.

'A masterpiece'
Derek Cooper

'Of the many books on our food, his is my favourite, the one I use most'
Jane Grigson

'The best book on the subject'
Giles MacDonogh, *Financial Times*

paperback